Christian, Lutheran, Confessional

How We Got to Where We Are

Arthur A. Eggert

In Terra Pax Lutheran Publishing
Sun Prairie, Wisconsin

Cover photograph: Lorchhausen am Rhein
                   Photograph by Joan Eggert

ISBN: 978-0-578-74705-7
Library of Congress Control Number: 2020916128

Table of Contents

The Author

Arthur Eggert has an extensive background in the physical and cognitive sciences. He received a PhD from the University of Wisconsin-Madison in analytical chemistry and taught chemistry at Duke University. For 41 years he was a tenure-track professor in the Department of Pathology and Laboratory Medicine at the UW-Madison and its Medical School. His research included the design of computer hardware and software, the flow of laboratory specimens and information in a medical environment, and the human-computer interface. Dr. Eggert concurrently served as the director of informatics for the clinical laboratories of the affiliated university hospital, eventually becoming the chief of the hospital's clinical pathology service and the administrative director of its clinical laboratories.

Arthur Eggert has been teaching biblical doctrine and church history classes in WELS churches in the Madison area for 30 years. He has served on the Self-Study Committee for WELS Ministerial Training Schools, the Western Wisconsin District Commission on Adult Discipleship and the Wisconsin Lutheran Seminary Governing Board. He currently is a member of the WELS Institute for Lutheran Apologetics. He is the author of numerous articles that have appeared in *Forward in Christ*, *What About Jesus* and the *Wisconsin Lutheran Quarterly* and has presented three pastoral conference papers. He is the author of *Simply Lutheran* (Northwestern Publishing House), a resource to strengthen the doctrinal understanding of Lutheran laypeople, and a co-author of *Clearing a Path for the Gospel* (In Terra Pax Lutheran Publishing), a book on Lutheran apologetics.

Reviewers and Commenters

The author wishes to thank those people who reviewed and commented on this book while in preparation for their valuable insights.

Rev. Jonathan Balge – Parish Pastor
David Becker – Attorney
Rev. Dr. John Brenner – Professor, Wisconsin Lutheran Seminary
Sharon Grinyer – Insurance Claims Adjuster
Anita Hahm – Christian Day School and Piano Teacher
Rev. Ronald Hahm – Professor, Luther Preparatory School
Rev. Geoffrey Kieta – Circuit Pastor
Rev. Paul Koelpin – Professor, Martin Luther College
Jane Kohlwey – Attorney
Patricia Horstmeier – Clinical Laboratory Administrator
Rev. Luke Werre – Parish Pastor

The author also wishes to express his deepest gratitude to his wife Joan and his daughter Emily Mandler for their many hours spent reviewing the text.

Introduction

For many Lutheran laypeople, the history of the Christian church is divided into three eras, namely, what happened in the Book of Acts, what happened during the Reformation, and what happened since they first began attending church. While they realize there were events which occurred between these eras, they assume that those events must not have been of great significance because pastors seldom mention them. If people or happenings from these obscure periods are brought up by anyone, they are quickly forgotten as unnecessary details.

The purpose of this book is to supply noteworthy information from the history of the Christian, i.e., New Testament, church in a manner that is not as long, dull, and detailed as are most books about history. This book is intended to be brief but to discuss key people and events with enough detail to aid the average layperson in appreciating the whys and wherefores of how we became Confessional Lutherans. It will review the Christian church from the time of Christ to our era. The title of the book refers to the three eras of which people have some knowledge, and the rest of the book will provide important specifics from the times between those high points.

As we proceed, we will consider key topics, that is, topics that were important in the development of Confessional Lutheranism as we know it today. The history of the Christian church is indeed long and involved, but knowing it in detail is not of much use in the daily life of the average layperson. Only scholars really need to know the particulars, and even they often only know them well in their limited area of interest. By way of contrast, our interests are more in the nature of "Where did that idea come from?" and "Why do we follow this practice today?" This might whet the reader's desire to learn more, or it might not, and that is okay too. The author is interested in improving the reader's gestalt (i.e., unified understanding) of his or her faith, not in attempting to transform the reader into a historian.

The book will also present many prominent figures in Christian history, that is, the people who are sometimes mentioned by those who are more educated in religious matters. By learning a small amount about these people, the reader will feel less at a disadvantage when references are made to them. Some of these historical Christians were much like us, while others were quite dissimilar from us. Some might even be regarded as outlandish.

Finally, the book will examine the real-world context in which these religious events occurred and in which these historical Christians lived. The Christian church threads throughout the growth and evolution of Western civilization, often influencing and being influenced by it. Looking at the history of the church in this context will make the church seem less like a spirit floating through history and more down-to-earth in terms of other events about which we are aware. Moreover, much of this historical period was anything but spotless, so informal language will sometimes be used to give a more realistic feel to the situations as they were experienced. The book begins with the whole Christian church, gradually narrows to Western Christianity, then to Lutheranism, and finally to Confessional Lutheranism as it proceeds to its conclusion. Confessional Lutherans accept the Lutheran Confessions as being true and binding as written, not merely as documents with historical significance.

There are many sources of historical information available today, particularly online and in scholarly tomes. They offer depth on specific topics, but seldom bring relevant people and events together to form a cohesive picture. Creating such a picture is the goal of this book. When the reader has finished it, the author hopes that the book will draw him or her back anytime there is a need to put the happenings in the church into perspective. We all fare better when we know where we came from. Theologically speaking, we do not want to return to the errors of the past.

Because this book is a condensed history of a portion of the Christian church and is intended for laypeople and not for scholars, references will usually only be given to more comprehensive works on church history rather than to the original documents or research articles. The bibliography contains works that have the numerous references which scholars need to pursue their work.

1

Apostolic Times

AD 30–100

St. Paul wrote, "When the set time had fully come, God sent his Son to be born of a woman, so that he would be born under the law, in order to redeem those under the law, so that we would be adopted as sons." (Galatians 4:4, 5) By this statement Paul meant that God the Father's choice of a time and a place to send his Son into the world to save people from the guilt of their sins was conducive to the spread of the message of that salvation. A brief look at the Roman world in the first century will show us that what Paul wrote by inspiration was consistent with what could be observed.[1]

The Roman World

The Middle East and the Mediterranean Basin had long been areas of warfare among the resident populations as well as against outside invaders, such as the Persians. By the time Christ was born, the empire founded by Rome had come to dominate the whole region. Although small local conflicts continued among the minor rulers in the empire and larger conflicts occasionally occurred between rivals for the throne in Rome, throughout the region there was a general sense of peace, which was referred to as the "Pax Romana" (the "Peace of Rome"). Rome's armies were too powerful for any rival in the Med-

---

[1] Philip Schaff, *History of the Christian Church*, Vol. 1 (Peabody, Massachusetts: Hendrickson Publishers, 1858/2002).

Gregory S. Aldrete, *The Roman Empire from Augustus to the Fall of Rome* (Chantilly, Virginia: The Great Courses Teaching Company, 2019), Lect. 1–4.

iterranean Basin or in the Middle East to challenge them. As a result, the citizens of the Roman Empire lived and did business in peace. Roman laws and justice, although often harsh, were, at least in principle, fair and consistent. Although the Jews hated their Roman overlords, many of the people in the empire were quite content with Roman rule. The alternative was frequent wars among local leaders, which devastated both commercial trade and the lives of the resident population. The general state of peace was an important factor in the spread of the Christian church.

The organization of the Roman Empire was not as simple as it is sometimes pictured. Within the empire there were numerous local languages and customs. Latin was the imperial language in the western parts of the empire, and it was necessary to speak it there to prosper. It was dominant among the peoples in what are now Italy, Spain, Portugal, France, England, and northern Africa westward from Tunisia. Greek, on the other hand, was the imperial language in the eastern portions of the empire. It was dominant among peoples in what are now the Balkan states, Greece, Turkey (often called "Asia Minor" during this period), Egypt, and the Middle East. Most educated Romans in the West spoke Greek as well as Latin, even though the Romans had conquered the Greeks. Moreover, most of the people in the Middle East spoke Aramaic as their business and social language, using Greek only in more formal situations or for official business. The widespread use of Greek enabled Christians across the empire to easily communicate with each other. That God choose to have the New Testament of the Bible written in Greek, therefore, makes sense from the viewpoint of communication.

The final characteristic of the Roman world which made it favorable for the spread of Christianity was the dispersal of the Jews (called "the diaspora") to many parts of the empire and beyond. Part of this scattering was the result of the Assyrian and Babylonian captivities of Israel and Judah. Through these captivities the Jews were moved as far east as Babylon, and from there many Jews had never returned. Other Jews had fled to Egypt at various times for safety. In addition, numerous Jewish entrepreneurs had moved into Syria, Asia Minor, Greece, and even Rome looking for business opportunities. The diaspora permitted the messengers of the Gospel to find people with the background necessary to understand their spiritual teachings nearly everywhere they went. While most of these scattered Jews did not accept the Christian message, there were often enough converts to form the nuclei around which new Christian congregations could be built.

Taken together, these factors strongly indicate that, even from a human perspective, it was a good time for beginning the Christian church.

The Great Commission

After his resurrection Jesus gave his final instructions to his disciples, but his time as the visible leader of his followers was nearing its end. Certainly, he was the perfect teacher. Still, like any teacher of his era, he was only able to work with a small group at any one time and then only when he was physically present with them. There were no mass media by which he could spread his teachings nor any rapid means of transportation that could carry him to distant locations. He needed to send out others to take his message throughout Judea, the Middle East, the Roman Empire, and beyond. He therefore gave his disciples the Great Commission, "Go and gather disciples from all nations by baptizing them in the name of the Father and of the Son and of the Holy Spirit, and by teaching them to keep all the instructions I have given you." (Matthew 28:19, 20)

To carry out this commission, Jesus's disciples, who became known as "apostles" from the Greek word meaning "sent," needed a lot more than just the information which they had learned in three years with Jesus. They needed the assurance that they were not going to be alone in this monumental enterprise of teaching everything about Jesus to everyone. To reassure them, Jesus promised that he would be with them with his sustaining and spiritual presence, even after his physical presence was withdrawn. He said, "Surely I am with you always until the end of the age." (Matthew 28:20) In addition, he promised to send the Holy Spirit, the third person of the Trinity, to guide them into a correct understanding of his teachings. He told them, "When the Counselor comes, whom I will send to you from the Father—the Spirit of truth, who proceeds from the Father—he will testify about me." (John 15:26) Armed with their God-given knowledge and this divine assurance, they readied themselves to undertake the world's greatest mission ever.

The mission commenced on the day of Pentecost, one of the three special festivals on the Jewish religious calendar.[2] All the men of Israel were to assemble in Jerusalem to celebrate this festival. Many Jewish men did come from across the Roman Empire for such festivals, even from as far away as

---

[2] The Feast of Pentecost was also known as the Feast of Weeks in the Old Testament and was described in Leviticus 23:15–21.

Rome itself, although the attendance never approached the "every Israelite male" as was required by the law given through Moses.[3] Nevertheless, on this particular Pentecost festival that occurred fifty days after the resurrection of Jesus on Easter, the Lord God poured out his Spirit on the assembled disciples. Their understanding of Jesus's message became considerably clearer, and their fear of the Jewish leaders receded. They were able to proclaim the message of salvation through Jesus Christ in a miraculous way so that all the people from the various parts of the Roman Empire could understand the message in their own languages (Acts 2). On this first day of the Christian church, the Holy Spirit brought three thousand men to faith. While the visible power which the Holy Spirit displayed on Pentecost was not a constant presence in the work of the apostles, it nevertheless drove their mission and produced continual fruit as time passed.

The Mission to the Jews

The church developed through the work of two missionary teams. Jesus had directed his followers to begin their work in Jerusalem.[4] Thereafter, they were to proceed to more distant fields.[5] And they did begin their work in Jerusalem, as mentioned in the previous paragraph, with spectacular results. The first few chapters of Acts describe the growth of the church and the work of key apostles such as Peter and John. The church grew so quickly and the members became so numerous, in fact, that it was soon necessary to put into place the beginnings of a management structure.[6] Things were looking favorable, but because the growth in the number of followers of Jesus was occurring so rapidly and was happening in the seat of Jewish power in Jerusalem, it began to trouble the Jewish religious leaders.[7] Along with the matter of the purity of their religion, there was a concern over the thrice-yearly influxes of Jewish pilgrims into Jerusalem. Jewish leaders might have legitimately feared that Jesus's followers would use one of these occasions to foment a revolt against

---

3   [The LORD said,] "Three times a year all your males shall appear before the LORD God." (Exodus 23:17)
4   [Jesus said,] "The Christ will suffer and rise from the dead on the third day, and repentance and forgiveness of sins will be preached in his name to all nations, beginning from Jerusalem." (Luke 24:46, 47)
5   [Jesus said,] "You will be my witnesses in Jerusalem, in all Judea and Samaria, and to the ends of the earth." (Acts 1:8)
6   Acts 6:1–7.
7   Acts 5:12–42.

the Romans and bring Roman retaliation upon the city. They began a program of persecuting the leaders of the church, including the stoning of the deacon Stephen.[8] With such a general persecution going on in Jerusalem, members of the church began to flee, seeking the relative safety of other cities in Judea and Samaria.[9]

In training the early church workers, Jesus had concentrated on creating a Jewish missionary team. In fact, initially he had told his followers to preach solely to the "lost sheep of the house of Israel" (Matthew 10:6). Indeed, the apostles and other early church teachers did concentrate on the Jews. The geographic mission field in which they were working was extensive, running from Alexandria in Egypt, through Palestine, Syria, and Mesopotamia, all the way to the area where once the great city of Babylon had stood. They were certainly linguistically well-prepared for this mission because they all spoke the Aramaic and Hebrew languages used by the Jews throughout this region. This meant that they could quote Jesus's words as he had spoken them.

The spread of the message in these areas near Judea was significant. Acts mentions such places as Samaria,[10] Caesarea,[11] Damascus,[12] and Antioch (Syria).[13] While some Jews in these places believed, resistance to the message also began to grow across this region. The Jewish religious leaders in Jerusalem could envision that as conversions to Christianity (as it began to be called) spread among the Jews of the diaspora, these Christianized Jews might form mobs and create problems in Jerusalem during the mandatory religious feasts. By claiming Jesus was "the Christ," that is "the Messiah," for whom the Jewish people had been waiting for centuries, the apostles were raising political as well as religious concerns for the Jewish leadership. These leaders, therefore, began to send their agents to cities outside Jerusalem to round up these "Christians" and bring them to Jerusalem to compel them to return to the Jew-

---

[8] Acts 7.
[9] "On that day a great persecution broke out against the church in Jerusalem, and all except the apostles were scattered throughout the countryside of Judea and Samaria." (Acts 8:1)
[10] "Philip went down to the city of Samaria and began preaching the Christ to them." (Acts 8:5)
[11] "Philip, however, found himself at Azotus. And as he went from place to place, he preached the gospel in all the towns until he came to Caesarea." (Acts 8:40)
[12] "There was a disciple in Damascus named Ananias." (Acts 9:10)
[13] "Now those who had been scattered by the persecution that took place at the time of Stephen traveled as far as Phoenicia, Cyprus, and Antioch, speaking the word to no one except Jews." (Acts 11:19)

ish faith or to execute them.[14] In addition, the Jewish establishment appealed to the local secular rulers, either Romans or their puppet local kings, to aid in the persecution of the Christians.[15]

Perhaps the Jewish religious leaders could have waited out the situation, hoping that the movement would fall apart when Jesus did not quickly return as his followers expected. The apostles, however, had been given miraculous powers for healing the sick and the disabled. These healings proved difficult to challenge.[16] Yet, due to the division among the various Jewish groups over doctrine and to the political games they had to play with the Roman authorities, they were not able to destroy the Christian movement, even in Jerusalem. Nevertheless, the Jewish religious leaders were successful in martyring numerous apostles and other church leaders. Legend says that all the apostles were martyred except for John, but there is insufficient evidence to validate this claim. Many of the apostles may have simply disappeared into the mission fields. We have no record of their work or how they died.

Beyond Jerusalem, the Jewish missionary team faced two problems in its work among the scattered Jews. The first was making sure that all members of the team were teaching the same information about Jesus and his ministry. In repeating the words and ideas of Jesus, those words and ideas might easily become corrupted. In fact, the likelihood of the message becoming corrupted was far greater than its remaining pure, at least from a human perspective. Addressing this problem led to the creation of a written record of the events and the message of Jesus's ministry. We do not know exactly when this process began or the procedure that was followed. Perhaps, the apostles discussed the problem and pooled their knowledge to produce the first written gospel. Certainly, the Holy Spirit guided their work. The book of Matthew, as we have it today, is probably the result of such an effort. The book portrays Jesus as the fulfilment of the Messianic prophecy and would have been exactly what the missionaries to the Jews would have needed to do their work. Matthew

---

[14] "Meanwhile, Saul was still breathing out murderous threats against the disciples of the LORD. He went to the high priest and asked him for letters to the synagogues of Damascus, so that if he found any men or women belonging to the Way, he might bring them to Jerusalem as prisoners." (Acts 9:1, 2)

[15] Acts 12:1–5.

[16] "After they had ordered them to leave the Sanhedrin, they discussed the matter among themselves. They asked, 'What should we do with these men? To be sure, it is evident to all who live in Jerusalem that a miraculous sign has been done through them, and we cannot deny it.' " (Acts 4:15, 16)

may have been the chosen writer because he had gained literary skills working for the Romans as a tax collector. Perhaps his book was first written in Aramaic and then translated into Greek. We simply do not know. In any event, it has always been positioned as the first gospel. It may well have been the first gospel written to meet the immediate needs of the Jewish missionary team.

The second problem that this missionary team faced was explaining to the Jews which parts of the teachings of Moses were still relevant and which parts were no longer necessary because Christ had fulfilled them. Some Jewish Christians wanted to keep all the regulations, while others wanted to toss out everything not directly related to the gospel. This included the requirement to show kindness to one's neighbors,[17] which is the essence of the second table of the Moral Law. The book of James and several councils of church leaders in Jerusalem[18] attempted to address this problem.

The work among the Jews as a separate activity from the work among the Gentiles continued throughout the first century, but it became more difficult as time passed. James, the leader of the church in Jerusalem, was martyred in AD 62.[19] A few years later a revolt broke out among the Jews, leading to the destruction of Jerusalem in AD 70. This further scattered the Jewish Christians from Jerusalem. Moreover, the destruction of the temple and much of the priestly class (i.e., the Sadducees) left the Pharisees as the dominant party in Judaism. They began a theological counteroffensive against Christianity to retain and regain Jews for Judaism. This resulted in the production of *The Mishnah*,[20] which was completed in approximately 200, with some parts available much earlier. Gradually, the Jewish Christians became integrated into the Gentile branch of the church, which was growing much more rapidly.

---

[17] "When you reap the harvest from your land, you are not to finish reaping all the way to the edge of the field. Do not gather up the gleanings of your harvest. Do not strip your vineyard clean, and do not pick up the fallen grapes from your vineyard, but leave them for the poor and the alien who live with you. I am the LORD your God." (Leviticus 19:9, 10)

[18] Acts 11:1–18 and Acts 15:6–29.

[19] All years given in this book are AD, unless otherwise specified. Dates having less than three digits and the first dates in a chapter will often have AD attached.

[20] Herbert Danby, trans., *The Mishnah* (Peabody, Massachusetts: Hendrickson Publishers, 2011).

The Mishnah contains the oral teaching tradition of the Jews which supposedly was given to Moses by God on Mt. Sinai and which was edited by rabbis, particularly of the Pharisees, and supplemented with practical examples.

The Mission to the Gentiles

Although the Jews were the focus of Jesus's earthly ministry, he did not completely exclude the Gentiles. He healed the daughter of a Syrophoenician woman[21] and the servant of a Roman centurion[22] because they had faith in him. His parable about the Good Samaritan[23] and his dealings with the woman at the well of Sychar[24] also showed that he had an acute interest in the neighboring peoples. Still, Jesus did not personally train a Gentile missionary team in the same manner as he had trained the Jewish missionary team. As a result, it was not always clear to the apostles as to how they were to approach the Gentiles.

God, therefore, began to nudge his church in the correct direction. Philip was told to join an Ethiopian official in his chariot to instruct him using the book of Isaiah.[25] Peter was sent, after being reprogrammed by a vision, to the home of a Gentile centurion named Cornelius.[26] The Jewish Christians in Antioch on their own started to teach the good news of Jesus to Gentiles.[27] All this created a stir among some Jewish Christians in Jerusalem because they did not understand that the message of salvation was for everyone.[28]

A central part of God's plan for a missionary team to the Gentiles was the Jewish Pharisee Saul.[29] He was an archenemy of the Christian church, but God brought him to faith.[30] After his conversion, he was led through a course of study directed by God himself to prepare him for his difficult assignment.[31] Starting at Antioch in Syria, Paul began his missionary journeys westward,

---

[21] Mark 7:24–30.
[22] Matthew 8:5–13.
[23] Luke 10:25–37.
[24] John 4:1–42.
[25] Acts 8:26–39.
[26] Acts 10.
[27] "But there were some men from Cyprus and Cyrene who came to Antioch and also began to speak to the Greeks, preaching the good news about the LORD Jesus." (Acts 11:20)
[28] Acts 15:1–5.
[29] Certainly, there was always crossover between the work of the Jewish and Gentile missionary teams. Paul, for example, regularly started his work in the local Jewish synagogue. Nevertheless, there was a difference in the thrust of their efforts, as Paul wrote, "They saw that I had been entrusted with the gospel for the uncircumcised, just as Peter was entrusted with the gospel for the circumcised." (Galatians 2:7)
[30] Acts 9:1–18.
[31] "But I want you to know, brothers, that the gospel I preached is not of human origin. For I did not receive it from man, nor was I taught it, but I received it through a revelation from Jesus Christ.... I did not go up to Jerusalem to those who were apostles before me. Instead I went away into Arabia, and then I returned again to Damascus." (Galatians 1:11–17)

first into Asia Minor and then into Europe.[32] He gradually attracted others (e.g., Barnabas, Silas, Mark, Luke, Timothy, and Titus) to join in the effort. As he traveled, he distributed these fellow workers among the various churches which he had founded. His general pattern was to start at the local Jewish synagogue and to preach Jesus as the promised Messiah.[33] Some Jews accepted the message; however, most did not and often drove the believers out of the synagogue. Paul then turned to the Gentiles in the community. Sometimes his work went peacefully, and sometimes it led to turmoil and riots.[34] Paul finally made it all the way to Rome,[35] but as a prisoner. He may even have traveled beyond Rome. In his wake, he left a series of congregations under the general guidance of his spiritual lieutenants and of the pastors and elders they had trained.

Paul also made a major literary contribution to the church through the many letters he wrote to Christian congregations and to individuals. These letters laid out Christian doctrine and practice. Thirteen of these letters became part of the New Testament. His letters were carefully collected, copied, and spread among the Greek-speaking congregations across the whole swath of the northern Mediterranean Basin. The Pauline Epistles are still a lynchpin in the teachings of the Christian church.

In addition to the gospel written by Matthew, gospels by other writers also recorded the history of Jesus's life. Mark seems to have been a messenger and a versatile member for the Christian missionary teams because he traveled to many congregations across both the Gentile and Jewish areas of the church. He wrote a gospel that has many similarities to that of Matthew, but it is shorter and less focused on the fulfilment of the Old Testament prophesies. It was tailored more toward the common people in Greek communities who were not familiar with the writings of the Old Testament. Luke, who was the writer of the book of Acts, also wrote a gospel. He was a physician,[36] and his attention to detail gained through his profession is evident in his writings. His gospel would have been more appealing to the better-educated Greek-speaking Christians. Finally, the Apostle John, who outlived the rest of the apostles,

---

[32] Acts 13–28.
[33] "Paul and Barnabas entered the Jewish synagogue and spoke in such a way that a great number of both Jews and Greeks believed." (Acts 14:1)
[34] Acts 17:5–9.
[35] "There we found some brothers and were invited to stay with them for seven days. And so we came to Rome." (Acts 28:14)
[36] "Luke, the dearly loved doctor, greets you." (Colossians 4:14)

wrote a gospel that emphasized important doctrinal matters of Jesus's teachings as they contrasted with the teachings of the Jewish leaders. The four gospels, the letters of Paul, and the book of Acts formed the core teaching material used by the Christian church at the end of the first century. Other books by apostles also existed at this time, but they had not yet been so widely circulated and accepted. These will be discussed in the next chapter.

Early Heresies

Heresies troubled the church from its very beginning. Many Jews who accepted Jesus as the Messiah struggled to break free of the requirements of the Law of Moses.[37] They wanted to mandate that all the Jews who joined the church be required to keep these laws. Some went further and also wanted the Gentile Christians to keep some or all the Mosaic requirements as a condition of salvation.[38] This latter group was referred to as "Judaizers," and they troubled the church in numerous places.[39]

As time passed, some in the church developed their own ideas about what the church should teach and challenged the church leaders. Other false teachers wormed their way into the church from the outside. As the church grew, these invaders sought to redirect the church and use it as a platform for their own ideas. The most significant of these groups will be examined in the next chapter, to see how they grew from minor nuisances to major threats to the church's existence. These errors often involved some form of mysticism,[40] work righteousness, or a combination of the two.

The Apostolic Fathers

As the apostles died, a leadership vacuum grew at the top of the Christian church, which by then stretched from Hispania to eastern Mesopotamia and beyond. The apostles had been responsible for the purity of the teachings of Christ because they had received the Holy Spirit and had the power, at least

---

[37] "Then they said to him [Paul], 'You see, brother, how many thousands there are among the Jews who have believed, and all of them are zealous observers of the law.' " (Acts 21:20)

[38] "Some men came down from Judea [to Antioch] and began to teach the brothers: 'Unless you are circumcised according to the law handed down by Moses, you cannot be saved.' " (Acts 15:1)

[39] Galatians 5:7–11.

[40] Mysticism is the supposed spiritual acquiring, through contemplation and self-surrender, of knowledge inaccessible to the intellect.

to a limited extent, to do miracles to validate their authority. With the apostles gone, who would fill their role in guarding the doctrine and guiding the practices of the church? The apostles had appointed a group of bishops and elders to succeed them, but most of these men did not have the stature and universal recognition of those commissioned directly by Jesus. Moreover, due to the inability to communicate rapidly over great distances, maintaining the uniformity of the church's teachings everywhere was a challenge.

Certainly, the new leaders of the church had the four gospels and the writings of Paul, but there was no formal program of religious training for the church's spiritual leaders. The leaders from this period of church history have subsequently come to be called the "Apostolic Fathers." Due to the difficulties of distance that they faced and the inherent tendency of people to refine things to their own liking, numerous spurious teachings in the church have been blamed on the leaders of this era. These will be discussed in later chapters.

It is perhaps good to consider several of the best known of the Apostolic Fathers. **Clement of Rome** (died AD 99)[41] was the Bishop of Rome near the end of the first century.[42] He is known as the writer of a letter to the congregation in Corinth, which is now called the *First Epistle of Clement*. He is thought to have known Paul and maybe Peter. **Ignatius** of Antioch (AD 35–110)[43] had probably known several of the apostles, including John, because Antioch was a very large city and was an important meeting place of the Gentile and Jewish branches of the church. Ignatius was sent to Rome to be executed but, on his way there, he wrote numerous letters that established his identity to later generations. He was particularly influential in the codifying of the church organization and of the power of the bishops. **Polycarp** of Smyrna (AD 69–155)[44] apparently was a disciple of the Apostle John and an early writer in the church. He, like many of the other Apostolic Fathers, was martyred by the Romans.

Two key documents which were influential in the church for centuries were written in the period of the Apostolic Fathers. A book entitled *Didache*[45]

---

[41] All dates are approximate because they have often had to be reconstructed from incomplete records.
[42] F. L. Cross, ed., "Clement of Rome, St.," *The Oxford Dictionary of the Christian Church* (New York: Oxford University Press, 2005).
[43] *David Hugh Farmer, "Ignatius of Antioch," The Oxford Dictionary of the Saints (New York: Oxford University Press, 1987).*
[44] F. J. Bacchus, "St. Polycarp," *The Catholic Encyclopedia* (New York: Robert Appleton Company, 1911).
[45] F. L. Cross, ed., "Didache," *The Oxford Dictionary of the Christian Church* (New York: Oxford University Press, 2005).

(from the Greek word for "teachings") was written late in the first century and contained instructions for Christian communities. These instructions covered Holy Baptism, Holy Communion, and church organization. The book was lost for many centuries, but a copy was finally found in the late nineteenth century.

The Shepherd of Hermas[46] was written in Greek in Rome early in the second century. The unknown author's position in the church is uncertain. It was widely used and was even considered to be part of the Bible by some. It, however, contains many heretical ideas, including one concerning the nature of the incarnation. The book subsequently fell out of favor.

The end of the Apostolic Period left the church in the hands of the disciples of the apostles but without a complete codification of the apostolic writings and without any organizational unity. In chapter two, which covers the next two centuries, we will see how this situation played out as the church grew numerically, faced more systematic persecution, and saw more forceful leaders stepping forward.

---

[46] John Chapman, "Hermas," *The Catholic Encyclopedia*, Vol. 7 (New York: Robert Appleton Company, 1910).

2

The Early Centuries of the Church

AD 100–300

After the time of the apostles, the Christian church spread throughout the Roman Empire and beyond its borders. By AD 250 Christians could be found across the area of the world known to Western civilization. There was no central church organization or training schools for clergy. The message was carried by those who had learned it from others, either verbally or by reading the writings of the apostles. With the destruction of Jerusalem in AD 70, any loyalty to the Jewish authorities disappeared. Christianity became more and more recognized as a separate religion rather than as another sect of Judaism.[1]

The Church Organizational

It was natural for the church outside Judea to spread more quickly in larger cities than in smaller villages. People gravitated to the cities for commercial advantage, and numerous philosophies and religions flourished within them. Cities were the marketplaces of ideas, as demonstrated by Paul's visit to Athens.[2] The spiritual leaders of the congregations in these larger cities came to

---

[1] Edward A. Engelbrecht, ed., *Church History: The Basics* (St. Louis: Concordia Publishing House, 2016), 1–35.

Schaff, *History of the Christian Church*, Vol. 2.

Kurt Aland, *A History of Christianity*, Vol. 1, trans. James L. Schaaf (Philadelphia: Fortress Press, 1985), 45–77.

Aldrete, *The Roman Empire*, Lect. 5, 6, 12–14.

[2] Acts 17:16–34.

be called "bishops."[3] Under the bishops were men who preached, men who taught, and men who carried out other churchly functions. Although originally called "elders," in many places these men came to be called "priests," probably because that was the title of the clergymen in Judaism and in the pagan world. As time passed, a more complex structure of church offices developed with multiple levels of clergy, particularly in the larger congregations.

As might be expected, many bishops came to prize their positions and power. When new congregations formed near an established congregation headed by a bishop, the established bishop often tried to assume authority over the new congregation as well. Conflicts, sometimes bitter, developed over the control of the geographical territory in which specific bishops exercised power. All bishops were nominally equal, but some were more influential due to the resources they controlled. Gradually, the bishops of four important cities moved to the head of the class and became known as "patriarchs" of their regions. The first such bishopric was, of course, Jerusalem. It was at Jerusalem where the church had started, and it was to it that in good times and bad the church looked for leadership. The influence of this patriarchy declined after the Roman destruction of the city left only a small number of Christians living in it and its vicinity. The second patriarchy was the bishopric of Antioch in Syria. Antioch was one of the largest cities in the empire and the crossroads of East and West. The third patriarchy was in Alexandria in Egypt. Alexandria was a city of scholars and the port for the Egyptian grain trade that fed much of the empire. The last patriarchy was in the city of Rome. Rome was prominent as the center of government and the place to which, it was claimed, all roads led. Patriarchs exercised a general influence over their geographical regions, but during this period they seldom had as much power as the patriarchs themselves might have desired.

The members of the clergy were selected by various systems, and these did not always produce good results. Elections for important church offices, such as bishop and elder, were common. In many congregations the process was generally orderly, with the bishop appointing his elders and other subordinates from qualified candidates and with one of the elders being chosen to succeed him as bishop. Unfortunately, sometimes the theological soundness of the candidates was ignored in favor of other factors, such as being popular and being able to speak well. Sometimes even popular non-Christians were

---

3   Philippians 1:1.

elected as bishops with the understanding that they would be baptized and ordained as priests before assuming the office of bishop. Other times, there was popular pressure to elect as bishop a man who was already the bishop of a nearby smaller bishopric, although such bishopric-hopping was generally frowned upon. Elders also sometimes attempted to move to more prestigious positions in bigger bishoprics. Elections to choose bishops in which all the members of the bishop's home church could vote continued for many centuries, even in such important bishoprics as Rome.

The Church Operational

Originally, membership in the church was given to anyone who attended church gatherings and claimed to believe. This approach soon led to difficulties because people with differing ideas of what the church should be and of what it should teach joined and tried to hijack congregations for their own purposes. We see this problem already in the letters to the seven churches in Revelation. Consequently, congregations gradually began establishing requirements for new members before they would be accepted as communicant members and given a voice in church affairs. These requirements included instruction in the faith, which often continued for one to two years. Because the congregations feared infiltration by government agents, particularly in times of persecution, adult proselytes[4] wishing to join a congregation needed faithful church members to act as their sponsors. A sponsor would vouch for the genuineness of the proselyte's intentions and watch over his or her instruction in the faith. The custom of sponsors continues today, but it is now usually honorary and generally only used for small children.

Everyone had to be baptized to become a member of the Christian church. Infants and young children could be baptized if at least one of their parents was a member of the church. The understanding in this circumstance was that the parent or parents would subsequently supervise the instruction of the child in the faith. Adults had to be instructed before baptism, as is now common. They also had to make a confession of their faith at the time of their baptism. That confession came to be called the "baptismal standard," and it varied from congregation to congregation. A standard that became popular in the Latin-speaking church was called the "Old Roman Symbol." After some refinement,

---

[4]   A proselyte is a new convert to the teachings of the church.

this standard developed into the Apostles' Creed. Some claimed that each apostle contributed a phrase to it, but this claim is without foundation. Today the Apostles' Creed is widely used as a confession of faith, but only in the Western branches of Christianity. The Greek-speaking churches and their successors in Orthodox Christianity never incorporated the Apostles' Creed into their liturgies.

Worship in the Christian church was initially patterned after the worship in the Jewish synagogue. As such, it consisted of readings that were taken from the Old Testament, the four gospels, and/or the writings of Paul. There were sermons to expound the Scriptures and the singing of psalms and hymns, as the latter were written. The Lord's Supper was celebrated. The liturgy was simple, without many of the now-common items. Worship was almost always held in private homes or converted synagogues, as churches were not built until after 250. In areas where there was persecution, Christians met in fields, caves, and catacombs.

Persecution

The persecution of the Christian church by the Gentiles during the second and early third centuries did not manifest itself in the form of a universal and continual attack on the church by the central government in Rome. It was rather the result of a variety of factors and happened at various times in various places. The Christians had initially been regarded as a Jewish sect. The Jews were hated because they refused to accept Roman gods and customs. From its very beginning, Christians inherited this Roman hatred for the Jews.

In addition, the Christians were considered secretive because they met in houses rather than in temples like the various pagan religions. While the Romans were generally tolerant of all religions, this secrecy caused many tales to surface about Christians performing unspeakable acts in their worship, such as sacrificing children, cannibalism, and abnormal sexual practices. These stories were widely accepted as true due to the preexisting ill will against the Christians.

Christians not only refused to worship the local gods of their communities, but they also refused to worship the emperor as a god. Emperor-worship had been started around the time of Christ as a way of unifying the empire. By burning incense to the emperor, people supposedly showed their complete loyalty to the Roman state. Failure to do so was considered by some to be treasonous. Christians refused to participate in such idolatrous rituals. Romans called Christianity a "superstition" and Christians "suspect" citizens.

Finally, Christianity attracted many slaves to its ranks. This made some Roman authorities apprehensive that the Christians were planning a rebellion fueled by the resentment of the slaves. When all this circumstantial evidence was added together, it was natural that Christians were viewed with suspicion.

Actual persecutions were usually triggered by local events. Nero found the Christians a convenient group to blame when the city of Rome burned in AD 64. Local rulers found persecuting Christians to be a way to gain favor or to shift blame when something went wrong. The Christians' failure to worship the gods was cited as the reason for bad weather, famines, earthquakes, and other ill fortune. It was not common that Christians were particularly sought out for persecution. However, if someone were discovered to be a Christian, he or she would become a scapegoat. If blame needed to be assigned and punishment to be administered, Christians were convenient victims. More systematic persecutions arose as the third century drew toward its close.

Slavery

Historically, slavery was an economic institution. The Mosaic Law permitted and regulated it. The slavery of an Israelite male or female was limited to six years of service,[5] but non-Israelites could be kept as slaves indefinitely. Children of slaves were slaves, unless adopted or emancipated. Jesus and his apostles said nothing to change this. In the Roman Empire slavery was harsher, at least in principle, because slaves had almost no rights. Yet, many slaves were well educated and held responsible positions in their communities. Some Christians, appreciating Christ's liberating them from the slavery of sin, came to view legal slavery in a negative light. Such Christians often released the slaves whom they personally owned. Because slavery was not race-based, a freed slave could easily blend into the general population as a "freedman," but this did not confer on him Roman citizenship. As St. Paul wrote, whether one was a free person or a slave[6] did not affect one's ability to be saved.

---

[5] Deuteronomy 15:12–18.
[6] "There is not Jew or Greek, slave or free, male or female, for you are all one and the same in Christ Jesus." (Galatians 3:28)

The Canon

For the church to survive, it was essential that every congregation taught the same message. If each congregation had had its own doctrine, then people moving from one area to another would have found that their new congregation was teaching something different than their old congregation had. Christians wanted to follow the truth, so how would they have known which teaching they should believe? Such doctrinal disunity would have made the church look unattractive to potential converts. The church, already under pressure from the Roman authorities and the Jews, would have dissolved into squabbling factions. To prevent this from happening, the Holy Spirit guided the church to recognize its need for a set of writings, comparable to those of the Old Testament, which would bind everyone to the same teachings.

The first writings to be included in this standard for teaching, which would become the New Testament, were easy for the churches to agree upon. The four gospels and the writings of Paul had been collected in many places, but particularly in the areas where they had been generated. The cities of Ephesus in Asia Minor and Antioch in Syria were centers for such collections. Both the Jewish and Gentile mission teams worked out of Antioch, particularly after Jerusalem was destroyed in AD 70. Paul, John, and other important church leaders spent time working at Ephesus. This meant that there were people available in these places who knew the writers and their styles and could discern which writings were genuine and which were imitations. Luke's Acts of the Apostles, the first epistle of John and the first epistle of Peter were also quickly recognized as works by these apostles. By the beginning of the second century, these twenty books were widely accepted[7] and quoted in the surviving writings of the church leaders of that era.

Other writings were more challenging.[8] People were curious and wanted additional details about Jesus's early life. They desired divine answers to numerous questions. This created a market, and suppliers of information to meet the demand soon appeared. There were those who were willing to tell fictious stories about Jesus and to write as authorities on subjects on which neither Jesus nor the apostles had ever spoken. To make such books more appealing, their authors often claimed that they were the work of an apostle or of one of

---

[7]   These books were referred to as "homologoumena."

[8]   William Hone, ed., *The Lost Books of the Bible* (New York: Bell Publishing Company, 1979).

their traveling companions. Examples are "The Gospel of the Birth of Mary," "The Gospel of the Infancy of Jesus Christ," and the "General Epistle of Barnabas."

Some of these numerous books at first appeared relatively similar to the twenty books which had quickly been accepted, while others read like racy short stories. Various arguments were made for and against the numerous books considered, and many of the books were soon discarded. Twelve remained and were referred to as the Antilegomena (i.e., the books spoken against). Of these, only seven were deemed to be of the same spirit with the other twenty books, namely, Hebrews, 2 and 3 John, 2 Peter, James, Jude, and Revelation. In each case, a major issue of concern was the genuineness of the authorship of the book. Eventually a large majority of the Christian leaders were satisfied regarding the legitimacy of these books. In the final analysis, the Bible is self-authenticating. It is the Holy Spirit working through the words of the various portions of the Bible that convinces the reader that they are indeed the words of God.

Heresies

Four major heresies troubled the church in this time period and continued to do so for the next several centuries. Certainly, they were not the only doctrinal challenges which the church faced in this era, but they were the most widespread and need to be understood.

Gnosticism comes from a Greek word meaning "having knowledge." Its origins are unclear, but it seems to have first arisen among Christian and Jewish thinkers of the first century. Its adherents emphasized personal spiritual knowledge gained from contemplation and from the wisdom that had been gained by the philosophers rather than the written Scriptures or the traditions of the Apostolic church. Gnostics taught that knowledge, often held only by the privileged, was the key to an abiding relationship with God. Their core belief was that there was a mind-spirit dichotomy, i.e., dualism. They minimized the need for an acknowledgement of sin and the necessity of repentance. Many Gnostics believed in a supreme god, called Bythos, who was good but remote. The creator of the world, on the other hand, was the evil Demiurge,[9] and there was a whole assembly of supernatural aeons[10] which personified vices and virtues, often muddling the world for mortals. The early church fathers, such as Irenaeus and Tertullian, wrote strongly against Gnosticism as being destructive to the apostolic doctrine of Christ as the fulfillment of the Old Testament prophecies. Opposing these orthodox teachers, **Valentinus** (100–160), who even sought to become the Bishop of Rome, claimed that Gnosticism was a fuller understanding of the Christian message. The Gnostic Christ was a divine being from the pantheon of the aeons who had taken on human form to lead man back to the supreme god, who was the source of true light. Another renegade to church doctrine, **Marcion** of Sinope, had some teachings similar to the Gnostics, but differed from them about the nature of the human soul. Gnostic ideas were not static and did not have the cohesiveness to survive against orthodox Christianity. They faded when Christianity became the dominant religion of the empire.

Manichaeism was founded by a Persian named **Mani** (216–274). It taught that there were both a great good god (The Father of Greatness) and an evil god (The Prince of Darkness) in the universe, neither of which was omnipotent. The battle between these gods took place through proxies, which included the human soul. The universe was the result of these forces employed in the battle. There was a spiritual world of light, where all light belonged, but that light had been scattered among the darkness of the evil material creation. For goodness to prevail, all light needed to be gathered and returned to the world of light. Manichaeism became a great world religion from the third through the seventh centuries, stretching all the way from the Atlantic Ocean to China. The establishment of Christianity as the only legal religion in the Roman Empire and the rise of Islam ended Manichaeism in the West. In eastern Asia it was gradually suppressed by various political rulers and eventually disappeared.

Montanism was founded by **Montanus** in the late second century in Phrygia in Asia Minor. Montanus was a relatively new convert to Christendom who believed that the Holy Spirit had spoken to him and had given him new prophecies which he was to proclaim to the world. He declared Pepuza and

---

9 "Demiurge" is a Greek word meaning "craftsman" or "artisan."
10 "Aeons" were subordinate divine beings that emanated from a superior central god. This term comes from a Greek word that means "time" or "age" and can mean "eternity."

Tymion in western Phrygia[11] to be the New Jerusalem. Montanus had two female companions named Prisca and Maximilla, who also claimed to receive direct revelations from the Holy Spirit. Having some teachings similar to Christianity, Montanism spread westward from Greece, through Italy and into Gaul. Because it relied on a connection being established directly between the worshiper and the Holy Spirit, the Christian church rejected the movement and its teachings. While it caused turmoil in some areas, it was gradually suppressed and disappeared in the sixth century.

Adoptionism taught that Jesus was born a human being but that he was adopted into the Godhead because of his stellar qualities and then commissioned to carry out the saving work for mankind. This idea appeared among the Apostolic Fathers in the book *The Shepherd of Hermas*, but it was championed during the third century by **Paul of Samosata** (200–275). Paul believed in **Monarchianism**, a teaching that God the Father was the real and supreme God, with the Son and the Holy Spirit being lesser divinities. That fit easily with adoptionism because it explained how the Son became a subordinate deity. In 260, Paul became Bishop of Antioch, one of the patriarchies of the church, but he was deposed by a gathering of fellow bishops in 269 for his false teachings and for his abuses of power. His ideas were refined by others in subsequent years, as will be discussed in chapter 3.

Many early heresies involved challenges either to the Trinity or to the nature of Christ and, as we shall see in subsequent chapters, there was significant overlap between the errors in these two central teachings.

The Great Theologians

The list of theologians who gained some fame during the second and third centuries could be long, depending on the criteria used to establish the list. Those making the list might not necessarily be the best churchmen of the era but would be those who had an impact that lasted long after their own era. In fact, from this period of church history, it is often those who caused the worst problems or who left a mixed legacy that are most remembered. Below are a few with whom the Lutheran reader may have some familiarity. While all of

---

[11]   Phrygia is in what is now western Turkey.

them contributed to the doctrinal clarification[12] in the church, they were not completely orthodox in their teachings.

Justin Martyr[13] (100–165)[14] was born in Samaria to a pagan family. He loved the study of moral philosophy. He started with Stoicism,[15] but eventually settled on Platonism.[16] An encounter with an old man expounding the Old Testament resulted in his conversion to Christianity. Justin then styled himself as a philosopher in both garb and manners. In Rome he opened his own school and attracted followers, but he was eventually beheaded for failing to burn incense to the gods. Justin emphasized an important doctrine of Christianity, namely that the Logos,[17] the second person of the Trinity, had to have existed before his incarnation. Most of his writings have been lost. What has survived strongly emphasizes moral behavior rather than saving grace.

Irenaeus (130–202)[18] was born in Smyrna in Asia Minor. He was raised in a Christian family and was a disciple of Polycarp, who had in turn been a disciple of the Apostle John. He traveled to Lyon, a city in the Roman province of Gaul (modern France). There he became a priest and then the bishop. He rigorously defended Christian orthodoxy, even exerting pressure on the Bishop of Rome in doctrinal matters. He emphasized the importance of reading the Scriptures in the churches. His most significant surviving writing is *Against Heresies* in which he traced the origin of the Gnostic heresy and contrasted it

---

[12] The doctrines of the Christian Church were all given directly by Jesus or by the Holy Spirit through the apostles. However, there were also a lot of false ideas being put forward by people who misrepresented the teachings that God had given. Some people genuinely did not understand the revealed teachings because their minds were mired in the ideas of the pagan world, and they mingled those ideas with Christian doctrine. Other introduced false ideas for their own purposes to gain influence and control in the church. It was necessary for the church leaders to clarify the correct teachings by separating them from the misconceptions and intentional false ideas. This took careful and determined effort to present the doctrines clearly without embellishment.

[13] He was named Justin at birth, and the designation "martyr" was added after his death.

[14] Karen O. Bullock, *The Writing of Justin Martyr* (Nashville: Broadman & Holman Publishers, 1998).

[15] Stoicism taught that the wise lived in harmony with the divine Reason and were indifferent to the fluctuations in fortune and to pleasure and pain.

[16] Platonism taught that abstract objects are ideal timeless entities, independent of the physical world and of the symbols used to represent them.

[17] Logos is the Greek word for "Word" in John 1:1. It was used in the early church as a technical term for the preincarnate Christ.

[18] Alexander Roberts and James Donaldson, eds., "Irenaeus Against Heresies," *Ante-Nicene Fathers*, Vol. 1 (Peabody, Massachusetts: Hendrickson Publishers, 2002).

with the real Christian teachings. He is considered a "saint"[19] by various branches of Christianity even though he was a millennialist.

Tertullian (155–225)[20] was probably a Berber[21] born in or near Carthage in northern Africa and was likely a lawyer. He converted from paganism to Christianity about 197. Many today regard him as the father of Latin Christianity because he wrote extensively in Latin before that was common. He wrote about discipline and morals, church organization, and apologetics[22] against both pagans and Jews. He often wrote polemically[23] and was strong in his condemnation of Gnosticism. Tertullian was the first to use the word "Trinity" among Latin writers, but his views about God were not biblically orthodox. He placed the Son and the Holy Spirit on a lower level than the Father. After a decade in the Christian church, he came under the influence of Montanism and was never made a "saint" in the western church.

Origen (185–253)[24] was born in Alexandria to a Roman father who was martyred for his Christian faith when Origen was seventeen. Origen studied Christianity and philosophy in the schools of Alexandria and became a recognized Christian scholar. He traveled widely around the Mediterranean region. Origen was a prolific writer, producing many books and biblical commentaries, including the doctrinal treatise *On the First Principles*. His most famous book was *Hexapla*, which contained two Hebrew and four Greek versions of the Old Testament. Although he helped codify Christian doctrine, he also supported many heresies. Origen's teachings included that Jesus's atonement was a ransom paid to Satan to liberate humanity. He also taught the preexistence of souls before creation and the ability of everyone to be saved if they went through a purging experience. Origen was enamored with allegory and used it as the basis for much of his biblical interpretation, setting a prece-

---

[19] The word "saint" is used here to indicate people officially held in high regard by the church.

[20] Alexander Roberts and James Donaldson, eds., "Writings of Tertullian," *Ante-Nicene Fathers*, Vol. 3, 4 (Peabody, Massachusetts: Hendrickson Publishers, 2002).

[21] The Berbers were a tribe native to western North Africa.

[22] Apologetics is providing reasoned arguments to justify something, typically a theory or religious doctrine.

[23] Polemics is the practice of making strong verbal or written attacks on someone or something in defense of one's ideas.

[24] Pope Benedict XVI, "Origen of Alexandria: Life and Works," *Church Fathers: From Clement of Rome to Augustine* (Vatican City: Libreria Editrice Vaticana, 2007), 24–27.

dent that has troubled the church ever since. He died after being released following two years of torture.

Marriage

The issue of marriage among both the clergy and laity began to trouble the Christian church during the second century and has continued to do so until today. Therefore, we need to spend some time considering the arguments raised. In the Old Testament the clergymen were married. This was essential because the priesthood was hereditary, so new priests could only be the sons of priests. Furthermore, Paul's statements concerning the qualifications for bishops and elders included their being married but having only one wife.[25] However, in the minds of many in the second century, these arguments did not settle the matter about whether the members of the clergy should be allowed to marry. People pointed to the example of Paul, who himself was not married. They argued that wives diverted husbands' attention from the work of the church to their home life.[26] They reasoned that owing to the dangers Christians faced, particularly the clergy, wives introduced unnecessary complications. Moreover, because the return of Christ was expected to be imminent, the urgency of proclaiming the message required not hindering the messengers with wives. As a result, there was a widespread effort to discourage marriage among the members of the clergy, particularly the higher levels of the clergy.

Another movement was beginning that played a role in the antimarriage sentiment. With the goal of becoming "more spiritual," some men isolated themselves by going to remote places and living there for extended periods. These "hermits" were highly respected in the church for their dedication. Naturally, marriage was not compatible with such a lifestyle. This lifestyle served as the forerunner of the monastic movement during subsequent centuries.

---

[25] "It is necessary, then, for the overseer to be above reproach, the husband of only one wife, temperate, self-controlled, respectable, hospitable, able to teach, not a drunkard, not a violent man but gentle, not quarrelsome, not a lover of money." (1 Timothy 3:2, 3)

"Such a man is to be blameless, the husband of only one wife, and to have believing children who are not open to a charge of wild living or disobedience." (Titus 1:6)

[26] "I would like you to be free from concern. The unmarried man is concerned about the things of the LORD and thinks about how to please the LORD. But the married man is concerned about the things of the world and thinks about how to please his wife, and so he is divided." (1 Corinthians 7:32–34)

Discouraging marriage for men, however, created a surplus of unmarried women. Houses were established for unmarried women who were willing to fully commit themselves to the LORD rather than to a husband. In the idiom of that era, therefore, the men of the clergy became married to the church while the women became "brides of Christ." The seeds of the convent system were being planted.

The marriage of laypeople also posed a challenge. Christianity included the Old Testament (the Hebrew Bible) as part of its Holy Scriptures, and the Mosaic Law defined the rules for marriage among God's chosen people. While most men had one wife or remained single, some men had more than one wife. Polygyny[27] was never specifically forbidden in the Old Testament, and God facilitated it in several instances.[28] A wife could be an "entitled" wife, with property rights for herself and her children, or a concubine, often a slave of the man or his entitled wife,[29] with restricted but clear legal rights.[30] In either case, the husband had a lifelong responsibility to provide for his wife or wives. Divorce was limited by the Mosaic Law[31] and sometimes forbidden.[32]

Marriage under Roman law was much different. A man could have only one wife at a time, but divorces were easy to get, and serial polygyny was accepted, at least in the upper classes. Concubinary was not recognized as such, but a man could take his slaves as mistresses with no legal restrictions and could buy or sell them at will.

The antimarriage sentiment in the church extended to the laity as well as the clergy. After all, it was argued, people's loyalty to Christ should reduce their need for spouses. An initially unofficial teaching that remaining single

---

[27] "Polygyny" (a man having more than one wife) and "polyandry" (a woman having more than one husband) are collectively called "polygamy."

[28] Jacob (Genesis 29:16–30), (David) 1 Samuel 25:37–44, (David) 2 Samuel 12:8.

[29] Genesis 30:3–12.

[30] In general, an "entitled" wife had the same social status as her husband, but a concubine had a lower status. A concubine was nevertheless regarded as an honorable member of a man's family, could not be sold, and had to be set free if she were divorced. Mistresses were regarded as prostitutes and not honorable for a man to have.

[31] "When a man takes a woman and marries her, if she is not pleasing to him because he has found something indecent about her, and he writes her a divorce document and hands it to her and sends her out of his house...." (Deuteronomy 24:1)

[32] "If a man finds a virgin who is not pledged in marriage and he grabs her and lies down with her and they are caught, the man lying down with her must give the father of the girl fifty pieces of silver, and she will become his wife. Because he violated her, he is not allowed to divorce her as long as he lives." (Deuteronomy 22:28, 29)

was a holier state than marrying gradually spread throughout the church and became generally accepted.

Moreover, if it was less holy for a man to have one wife, his having more than one was considered evidence that his heart was guided by lust rather than love. Furthermore, it was argued, Roman law could not be used to enforce the rights of concubines, so Christian men should not acquire them. Conversely, Christian women who had become concubines through the actions of others could remain so honorably. The church tried to buttress its position with various philosophical arguments, such as: a) If one wife divided a man's attention from the LORD, multiple wives would make the situation worse; b) Every man should be ready to be called to serve in the ministry from which he would be excluded if he had more than one wife; c) Tertullian argued that when people married their souls became merged for eternity, so polygyny and remarriage after the death of a spouse was impossible; d) Some claimed that the apostles had forbidden it, but they had forgotten to record the prohibition in writing; e) Allegorically, God had created only one wife for Adam (i.e., Eve), and Christ has only one bride, the Church. Although church leaders agreed that polygyny and concubinary were not, in general, desirable arrangements, the exact degree of prohibition was argued until the time of the Reformation and beyond.

As the third century dragged on, the issues that would define the genuine Christian church were coming to a head, as we shall see in the next chapter.

3

The Christianization of the Empire

AD 300–400

It was not a smooth transition from the era in which the bishops held strong in control of a scattered church to the era when the church began to gain more organizational unity. The transformation happened due to issues of doctrine and to the changing relationship between the church and the secular government.[1] Church-state issues will be a constant theme in subsequent chapters.

The Struggle for Control in the Empire

From the time of the murder of Emperor Severus Alexander by the Roman army in 235 until 284, there were twenty-three emperors. Only one emperor reigned for more than ten years, and almost all of them were murdered. This created instability in the empire, and it made consistent governmental policies impossible. It permitted the Germanic tribes to cross the Roman borders with increasing frequency–to raid, to settle in, and eventually to claim dominance over parts of the empire. The Roman legions were more and more populated by foreigners whose commitment to Roman ideals was lukewarm.

Beginning in 284, the empire was effectively split into two empires. One consisted of a Latin-speaking western half and the other of a Greek-speaking

---

[1] Engelbrecht, *Church History*, 36–89.
   Schaff, *History of the Christian Church*, Vol. 3.
   Aland, *A History of Christianity*, Vol. 1, 77–212.
   Aldrete, *The Roman Empire*, Lect. 15, 16.

eastern half. In each half there was a senior emperor titled "Augustus" and a deputy titled "Caesar." The deputy was to succeed the emperor when he died or retired. This was a poor idea that never worked well. There was jealousy among the principals in the arrangement. After a few untimely natural deaths in the western part of the empire, Constantine the Great became the western emperor in 306 and eventually reunited the entire empire under his rule.

The Growing Persecution of Christians

Periodic large-scale persecutions had occurred about every thirty years from the time of Nero in AD 64 until the period of increasing instability began in 235. The Christians were easy people to blame for the growing signs of decline in the empire. Many regarded the Christians as traitors who were undermining the empire by not worshiping its gods. For the emperors and their lieutenants throughout the empire, it was rarely a political mistake to kill or torture local Christians for the "common good of the state." Moreover, because the Christian population continued to grow, many Romans feared that they would give aid and comfort to those who might invade the empire from Germany or Persia. Persecutions became increasingly severe and widespread before Constantine came to power in the West. In fact, the era of Diocletian and Galerius has been labeled the "Great Persecution." Persecutions became empire-wide, and many Christian manuscripts were burned. This situation did not improve until Constantine won control of the whole empire.

The Donatist Controversy

In North Africa, the persecution of the church led to ultra-pious Christians who called themselves Donatists,[2] after Donatus Magnus, a Christian bishop probably of Berber descent. During the persecutions some Christians had surrendered their copies of the Scriptures to the governor, and some had even burned incense to the emperor. The Donatists insisted that those who had done such things could never be forgiven by the church and readmitted to it. They could be forgiven by God alone. In addition, the Donatists claimed only sacred acts, e.g., Holy Baptism, which had been performed by faithful priests were valid before God. Sacred acts done by hypocrites or those without a ped-

[2] John Chapman, "Donatists," *The Catholic Encyclopedia,* Vol. 5 (New York: Robert Appleton Company, 1909).

igree running back through a continuous line of faithful bishops were invalid. These acts needed to be repeated by those priests who were true believers and had such a pedigree. The Donatists ignored the fact that it was impossible to inspect people's hearts to see which of them truly were faithful believers. If the Donatist rules had been followed, even the Apostle Peter would have been forever excluded from the church after he denied his LORD three times. Donatism began to decline after the Roman Empire became officially Christian under Emperor Theodosius. It ended after the arrival of Islam.

Constantine the Great

Constantine (272–337)[3] was born in Serbia, the son of a Roman army officer with a similar name. His father rose to become the deputy ruler of the western empire in 293. Constantine was sent to the eastern part of the empire and rose through the ranks to become a military tribune, i.e., a senior officer. When his father became Caesar in the West in 306, he called Constantine to lead the Roman armies in Britain. After his father died the next year, Constantine was declared Caesar by his troops. He headed for Rome, but it took several years to arrive there it because he had to eliminate other claimants to the throne along the way. In 324 he defeated Licinius, the ruler in the East, and became emperor over both parts of the empire. As emperor, Constantine strengthened the governmental infrastructure and issued a new coin, the solidus, which remained the basis for the currency in both the East and the West for a thousand years. He reestablished Roman control of its frontiers.

Constantine believed that he had been victorious in the Roman civil wars because he had received a call from the Christian God through the sign of a cross that he had seen in the sky. Adopting the cross as his emblem, he marched on to victory. He then legalized Christianity in the empire, thereby ending most persecutions. In fact, he wanted to use Christianity to help him unify his empire and feared that heresy would bring God's wrath. When he learned that there was a dispute within the church over the nature of Jesus, he called the first of the church-wide councils to settle the matter (see the First Council of Nicaea below).

Although he discontinued the use of pagan symbols and introduced Christian symbols into the Roman government, Constantine was not consistently

---

[3] Timothy Barnes, *Constantine: Dynasty, Religion and Power in the Later Roman Empire* (Oxford: Blackwell Publishing, 2011).

Christian in his behavior for most of his life. Only during the last several years before his death did he become a catechumen in the church. He was not baptized until he was on his deathbed.[4] Despite this, he intervened to settle several church disputes.

As well as legalizing the Christian church and calling the First Council of Nicaea, Emperor Constantine is known for founding of the city of Constantinople[5] on the site of Byzantium as the new capital of the Roman Empire. The eastern half of the empire, where Constantine had grown up, was richer than the western half. Despite the excellent system of Roman roads, the empire was becoming undefendable due to its size. The loss of Britain and/or Gaul to the empire was far less critical than the loss of Egypt or Asia Minor. It therefore made political sense to shift the capital of the empire eastward into what had become its critical heartland.

Constantine's other enduring accomplishment was establishing a date on which to celebrate Christ's birth. Christians were not certain of the actual date. Constantine decided to set it at the same time as the winter solstice so Christians could celebrate something other than the pagan winter festival.[6]

The Dispute over the Nature of God and Christ

The widespread church, which lacked a unifying structure under the bishops, gradually developed theological differences in the second century. These intensified in the third century as ideas from Gnosticism, Manichaeism and Montanism became influential in various regions and congregations. Some bishops did not have sufficient understanding of the Scriptures to interpret doctrine, so men of clever minds and strong wills were able to influence the masses, even if they were not bishops. The most dangerous issues troubling the church involved the nature of God and the person of Christ. These matters had already arisen in the first century, but by the end of the third century, they were threatening to splinter the church.

---

[4] Many people postponed their baptisms in this era because they believed that Holy Baptism only forgave sins committed before it was administered and that they would have to do penance for sins committed after baptism. They postponed baptism so they would be liable for less penance before their death.

[5] Now the Turkish city of Istanbul.

[6] A date near one of the Jewish festivals is more likely because Bethlehem was near to Jerusalem to which Jews had to make a pilgrimage for three festivals each year. Stopping at Bethlehem to register would have been a natural act. This would also explain their traveling when Mary was on the verge of giving birth.

The central issue was the internal structure of God. Everyone agreed that there was a "Father" in the Godhead, but his nature was disputed. The Gnostics taught that the God of the Old Testament was the evil Demiurge, who was hardly a father figure to humankind. Although most Christians rejected Gnostic ideas, the relationship of the Father to the Son and the Holy Spirit was the subject of many different false teachings. Were all three persons in the Godhead equal, or was there some sort of hierarchy? Were all three persons eternal, or was the Son a creation of the Father? Was the Holy Spirit a person or just an expression for God in action? Was there only one person in the Godhead who wore different masks, like actors in a Greek play, when he acted in different roles? Around the Mediterranean Basin, ideas and arguments about the internal structure of God were abundant, although these appear to have been more common in the eastern part of the empire than the western part at the beginning of the fourth century.

If the nature of the Trinity were in doubt, eventually the nature of Jesus would also be doubted. Was he both truly God and truly man, or was he something else? Was the Son eternal like the Father? If not, was he created at some point in time before the birth of Jesus, and if so, what was his relationship to the Father? Was Jesus adopted into the Godhead because of his blameless character? Was Jesus God at all or merely a man filled with the Holy Spirit? Was Jesus human, or was he only God with a disposable layer of flesh wrapped around his godly nature? How were the divine and human natures joined? The number of ways that these issues could be framed was mind-boggling. It is small wonder that Emperor Constantine wanted them settled before the newly recognized Christian church devolved into warring factions.

Arianism

The history of **Arius** (256–336) is hard to trace because Constantine ordered that his writings be burned. Much of the other information about him may have suffered the same fate. He was a Berber from Alexandria in Egypt, although he may also have studied in Antioch in Syria. He was ordained a deacon, but he was subsequently excommunicated by the bishop of Alexandria in 311. The next bishop, however, made him a presbyter[7] after restoring him to the church in 313. He was apparently of distinguished appearance,

---

[7]   "Presbyter" was the local designation for a priest.

well-mannered, and a good speaker. This attracted many laypeople to his cause.

Arius argued that the Son was not equal to the Father and was not eternal. The Son was the first of the Father's creatures and given divine status so that he could create the world and save it. He, however, was not of the same substance as the Father and was subordinate to him. The Arian heresy followed on the heels of previous heresies about the nature of God and allowed them to shelter together to build a larger following. Numerous bishops therefore initially were sympathetic to his ideas. There was a strong possibility for a substantial period of time that his ideas would prevail in the church as it was pressed by other religious movements. However, Arius was already an old man by the time of the Council of Nicaea and was no longer able to energetically campaign for his position, although others certainly did.

The First Council of Nicaea (325)

The First Council of Nicaea[8] was called by Emperor Constantine to resolve the issues dividing the Christian church, particularly regarding the status of God the Son in his relationship to God the Father. It also was to settle the method of computing the date of Easter. This gathering has been subsequently referred to as the first of seven great church councils. These councils were called "ecumenical" because they included representatives from across Christendom. This is somewhat of an exaggeration because all areas of the church were not always represented in the various councils. Nevertheless, the decisions of the councils for the most part became the accepted standard of doctrine throughout the Christian ("catholic") church. For this first council, all eighteen hundred bishops of the Christian church were invited, but only about three hundred attended.

The leaders of the two contending sides in the debate over whether the Son was begotten of the Father (and therefore of the same eternal substance as the Father) or whether the Son was a creation out of nothing by the Father were both from the church in Alexandria. On one side was Alexander I, the patriarch of the church in Alexandria.[9] His aide in arguing for the orthodox posi-

---

[8] Henry R. Percival, ed., "The First Council of Nice," *The Seven Ecumenical Councils of the Undivided Church* (Peabody, Massachusetts: Hendrickson Publishers, 2004), 1–57.

[9] Alexandria was often called the "See of St. Mark," who had, according to legend, founded the church there.

tion was a deacon named Athanasius, who would become his successor as Patriarch of Alexandria. They claimed that the Son was *homoousios* ("of the same substance") with the Father. Arius, a presbyter from Alexandria, argued that the Son was only *homoiousios* ("of similar substance") with the Father and therefore had to have been created by the Father. Emperor Constantine himself presided at the discussions. In the end, a substantial majority of the bishops agreed with Patriarch Alexander. Only two bishops sided with Arius and failed to yield to the majority. These three men were excommunicated and exiled to the western Balkans.

The Council of Nicaea is most remembered for drafting the first formulation of the Nicene Creed. This version of the creed contained little on the work and nature of the Holy Spirit because this was not an issue before the council. The council also separated the calculation of the date of Easter from the Jewish calendar, but it could not get all the bishops to adhere to a common way of determining that date. The problem of having different dates for Easter has persisted until today. Finally, the council created a detailed set of rules for the organization and operation of bishoprics in an attempt to gain uniformity and end petty disputes.

Athanasius

Athanasius (296–373)[10] was born into an upper middle-class Christian family in Egypt. He was given a good religious and secular education. His first theological work, *Against the Heathen*, was written when he was only about twenty years old. He soon thereafter became secretary to the Patriarch of Alexandria. He quickly became a deacon and traveled to Nicaea, where he distinguished himself in debate and even coined the critical word *homoousios*.

When the Patriarch of Alexandria died, Athanasius, over his own strong objections, was unanimously elected to replace him, even though he was only thirty years old. Athanasius sensed what was going to happen. Politics were going to become involved in the church. Why? Arius did not disappear in his exile. His supporters began recruiting bishops who were lukewarm in their support for the Nicene Creed at Nicaea or who had not bothered attending the council. The Arians recruited dissidents with other views on the nature of the Son or of the Holy Spirit to join their rebellion against the decisions of Nicaea.

---

[10] John Chapman, "Doctors of the Church," *The Catholic Encyclopedia*, Vol. 5 (New York: Robert Appleton Company, 1909).

They were able to get Arius's banishment lifted and began bringing charges of criminal behavior against Athanasius.

Over the next forty years, events became incredibly messy. Five times Athanasius was driven out of his See[11] at Alexandria, and numerous councils and courts were convened to examine the charges against him. He was excommunicated by councils, deposed by other bishops, exiled by emperors, and relentlessly pursued by the Arian faction. Nevertheless, in 366, the Bishop (Patriarch) of Rome called a council that declared no bishop's ordination was valid unless he accepted the Nicene Creed. The emperor yielded and allowed Athanasius to return to Alexandria as patriarch for the last seven years of his life. Although Athanasius had nothing to do with the writing of the Athanasian Creed, his determination to uphold the doctrine of the Trinity made the creed possible.

Constantine's Mother in Palestine

Constantine's mother Helena was not of noble birth and her legal relationship with Constantine's father is uncertain. After Constantine's father began advancing in his career, he sent Constantine and his mother to the eastern part of the empire while he continued his career with a different wife in the West. After Constantine himself was established as Augustus in the West many years later, he brought his mother into the highest circles of Roman power and had her given the royal title "Augusta" in 325.

Helena traveled to Palestine with full imperial backing during the period of 326–328 to seek relics of Jesus. She found numerous places that, at least according to local legend, were associated with Jesus's life and death. She ordered churches to be built at those sites which she thought to be most important. She found what she believed to be the "true cross," as well as the nails used to crucify Christ. She had no training in archeology, so she may in some cases have set future Christianity on a path to worship at places that were not what she claimed them to be. Her findings of "relics" certainly encouraged others to also seek "relics" that could somehow be linked to Christ. Without documentation of the genuineness of such relics, this soon became a game among adventurers and forgers which plagued the church well into the age of the Renaissance.

---

[11] A "See" is the home church (cathedral) of a bishop from which he exercises his power.

Constantine's Successors

To prevent the chaos and infighting that had preceded him, Constantine tried to make the office of emperor hereditary. He willed the joint rule of the empire to his sons Constantine II, Constans and Constantius[12] after his death in 337. While the brothers generally cooperated peacefully, there were disputes over the control of the church. With the death of Constantine II in 340, the empire was again split between East and West by the remaining two brothers. After the death of Constans in 351, Constantius temporarily reunited the empire under one-man rule until his death in 361.

The empire remained too unwieldy for one man to rule, however, so the emperor in Constantinople was forced to place an assistant in Rome. This power-sharing was often far from perfect. Julian the Apostate in Rome tried to reintroduce paganism as the only religion in the West, but he made few permanent gains for the pagan cause before his death in 363. After that, Christianity was in unchallenged ascendency in both halves of the empire, but the empire itself was falling apart. Germanic tribes took over *de facto* control of large portions of Gaul in the West, and the Persians wrested control of the Roman section of Mesopotamia from the empire in the East.

The problems in the empire had reached a desperate state when Theodosius became emperor in the east in 379. There was an ongoing struggle not only with progressive invasions by various Germanic tribes, but also a power struggle between Constantinople and Rome. Theodosius reunited the empire for the last time in 394. He made Christianity the state religion and soon thereafter died. By 400 Germanic tribes in the West were overrunning Gaul, and the emperor in the West was greatly limited in the control he could exercise outside of Italy. The grandeur of Rome was a thing of the past.

The First Council of Constantinople (381)

The persistence of the Arian heresy remained a threat to the Christian church, so Emperor Theodosius called another council in 381.[13] In fact, for years the patriarchy of Constantinople had been in the hands of the Arians, and the Patriarch of Antioch was sympathetic to them. The emperor, however,

---

12   Constantine was not known for his modesty!
13   Henry R. Percival, ed., "The First Council of Constantinople," *The Seven Ecumenical Councils of the Undivided Church* (Peabody, Massachusetts: Hendrickson Publishers, 2004), 161–190.

was in no mood to tolerate Arian Christianity and forced the Patriarch of Constantinople to resign. He then called a general council of the church to meet in his hometown. Only the bishops from the eastern portion of the church came, and a struggle ensued when Arian bishops were excluded from the assembly. The Patriarch of Antioch died suddenly, and a struggle over the high church offices in Antioch and Constantinople resulted. The orthodox bishops at this council, with the backing of the emperor, defrocked the followers of Arianism and turned their offices over to orthodox Christians.

Theologically, the council strengthened the Nicene Creed by rewriting the third article to firmly declare that the Holy Spirit was God and the third person of the Trinity. The doctrine of the Holy Spirit had only been lightly considered by the Council of Nicaea because it had not been regarded as a critical issue. Between the councils, challenges to the Holy Spirit being God had increased, causing the issue to be addressed at this council. The acceptance of the Nicene Creed in its revised form was made a requirement for holding any church office and for receiving protection under the empire as a Christian. As a result, numerous Arians fled the empire and carried their message to the Germanic tribes. Arianism among these tribes continued for several centuries and was brought back into the western portion of what had been the Roman empire.

The Great Theologians

Most of the notable theologians of the fourth century were in some way involved in the Arian controversy and/or the religious politics that had begun with Constantine legalizing Christianity in the empire. Their stories show the difficulties that befall faithful Christians in troubled times. With the changing political winds, they could be running their local congregation one day, be exiled or be on the run the next day, and be rehabilitated a few days later. Historians often struggle to understand exactly what happened that caused the various changes which plagued the lives of these churchmen. It is small wonder that many of them did not want the high offices for which their supporters put them forward. We will look at only a few as representative of the men who, like Athanasius, led the church through this difficult era.

Ambrose (named Aurelius Ambrosius at birth, 340–397)[14] was born into a Christian family in northeastern Gaul. He received a good general education

---

[14]   F. Homes Dudden, *The Life and Times of St. Ambrose* (Oxford: Clarendon Press, 1935).

because his father was in government service. He held minor government posts in Rome, where his talent was recognized. In 372 he was appointed governor of Liguria and Emilia with his headquarters at Milan. He remained in this position until he was elected Bishop of Milan in 374. This happened due to his popularity with the people, even though he was not theologically trained or even baptized! Becoming bishop put him in a position of significant power because the capital of the western Roman Empire had functionally been moved to Milan in 286.[15] Ambrose's relationship with the various emperors soured due to the efforts by the Arians to either oust him or acquire some of the church property in his bishopric. He steadfastly resisted surrendering anything to the Arians. He finally prevailed in his struggles when Theodosius gained control over the entire empire. Nevertheless, Ambrose had to discipline Theodosius for his senseless massacre of 7000 people at Thessalonica in 390.

John Chrysostom (340–407)[16] was born and educated in Antioch. He became a deacon in the church during the period of struggle between the orthodox Christians and Arian Christians for control of the church in that city. When orthodoxy prevailed, he became a recognized church leader and helped resolve disputes among patriarchies in Antioch, Rome, and Alexandria. He favored a literal interpretation of the Scriptures in contrast to the allegorical school of interpretation introduced by Origen in Alexandria. He also was active in the development of the eastern church's liturgy. In 397, he was chosen as Patriarch of Constantinople. He continued his efforts to reform the organization of the church while in Constantinople. He was not held in high regard by those with political power who felt he catered to the common people. He was exiled in 405 for reasons that are unclear, but which probably involved religious politics in the new Roman capital.

By the end of the fourth century, the Roman empire in the West was tottering, and the lights of intellectual knowledge were going out. This bleak period during which the western empire became partitioned among the Germanic tribes will be explored in the next chapter.

---

[15] Rome was a decaying city by this date with heavy urban pollution. It was hot and uncomfortable in the summers, causing the rich and powerful to flee to country villas anyway.

[16] Robert Wilken, "John Chrysostom," *Encyclopedia of Early Christianity*, ed. Everett Ferguson (New York: Garland Publishing, 1997).

4

The Collapse of the Western Empire

AD 400–600

By the beginning of the fifth century, the western part of the Roman Empire was in deep trouble.[1] Germanic tribes were moving into Gaul and staking out areas of influence. Nominally Roman legions were being led by Germanic generals. Visigoths, Vandals, Franks,[2] and numerous other tribes were vying for territory. Most of the trustworthy Roman legions had been pulled out of Britain. Romans in Hispania (Spain and Portugal) were also coming under intense pressure from the Germanic tribes. The Ostrogoths and the Huns were trying to cut the empire asunder by attacking in the Balkans. Even Italy was no longer safe from raids. The imperial court was forced to move from Milan to Ravenna in 402. The first sack of Rome was only a few years away.

Against the background of this growing danger, the church at Rome strove to solidify its power over the orthodox Christians in the West. This was made more difficult because many members of the German tribes that were progressively encroaching into its territory were Arians. Although persecution by the empire had ended, the church faced numerous difficult problems. It needed to assimilate all the people forced into it when Christianity was made

---

[1] Engelbrecht, *Church History*, 36–89.

　　Schaff, *History of the Christian Church*, Vol. 3.

　　Aland, *A History of Christianity*, Vol. 1, 215–275.

　　Aldrete, *The Roman Empire*, Lect. 19–22.

[2] The Visigoths, Vandals, Franks, Lombards, and Ostrogoths were all Germanic tribes. The Huns were a central Asian tribe.

the state religion. It faced determined opposition by some pagans who were strongly opposed to conversion. It had to deal with the remnants of prior heretical movements and, of course, there were the Germanic Arians. The church strained under this heavy load, but it slowly gained ground in its various struggles. Sadly, in the process of addressing these problems, new heretical ideas were introduced which would plague the church for centuries.

After this point in history, the Bishop/Patriarch of Rome was generally referred to as the "pope," a word derived from the Latin word for "papa." The other patriarchs were also sometimes called "pope," but to prevent confusion in this book, they will continue to be referred to as "patriarchs." We will start our examination of this period of Roman collapse by considering an institution that became a bulwark of the Western church. We will then introduce the men involved in the greatest religious controversy of the era being played out upon this troubled stage.

Monasticism

Monasticism grew out of the traditions of the Christian hermits in the Eastern church, who went to remote places to practice their faith through asceticism. At the end of the fourth century, ascetic practices made their way to Rome and then spread northward through Gaul into the British Isles. At first, men (called "monks") who undertook this lifestyle were free to come and go as they chose. Individual groups of monks adopted rules to govern their communal life.

Benedict of Nursia (480–543) was instrumental in systematizing monastic life in Catholic Church and became known as "the Father of Western Monasticism." Although educated in Rome, he opted for the life of a hermit in a cave outside the city. With a group of followers, he subsequently established the monastery of Monte Cassino between Rome and Naples. It was there that the Rule of St. Benedict was developed to regulate the activities of the monastery, its officers, and their responsibilities. This rule was later adopted by most other groups of monks and become the standard of monastic life for centuries.

To show their commitment to the ascetic life, monks were required under the Rule of St. Benedict to take vows of poverty, chastity, and obedience to their monastic order. Monastic life in the Middle Ages consisted of prayer, reading, and manual labor. Apart from prayer, which was the first priority, monks performed various tasks, such as preparing medicine, illustrating manuscripts, reading, and working in the gardens or on the land. Some monasteries had a scriptorium where monks wrote or copied books. The monasteries became the central storehouses of knowledge.

The Great Theologians

Jerome (347–420)[3] was born as Eusebius Sophronius Hieronymus in what is now Bosnia but at the time was the Roman province of Dalmatia. He moved to Rome as a young man and lived the wild lifestyle that was common among students in his and later eras. He was eventually baptized, began his theological studies in France, and then moved eastward through Greece and Asia Minor. He spent some time living as a hermit but eventually moved to Antioch. He then proceeded to Constantinople and finally returned to Rome. During this odyssey he became a scholar in Latin, Greek, and Hebrew.

In the middle 380s he became attached to the papal community and was asked to improve the Latin translation of the Bible. The Latin Old Testament in use was a translation of the Greek Septuagint, which was itself a translation of the Hebrew Bible. This translation project would occupy him for the next twenty years. Jerome soon left Rome and went to Palestine, which he found much more suitable for the strict ascetic religious life that he now advocated. Working directly from the best Greek and Hebrew sources available, in 405 he finished a new Latin translation. This became known as the *Vulgate*[4] and was the official Bible of the Roman Catholic Church for fifteen centuries. Jerome spent the rest of his life writing Bible commentaries. He died in Bethlehem in 420.

Pelagius (354–418)[5] was born in the British Isles and was of Celtic origin. He was well versed in Latin, Greek, and theology. He moved to Rome and initially found favor in orthodox Christian circles there. He was, however, deeply committed to asceticism. He increasingly objected to what he viewed as the loose lifestyles of the Roman Christians and to how easily they could be forgiven for their sins. He blamed this on the view of divine grace for the individual that was taught by theologians such as Augustine and Jerome. He considered this readily available forgiveness as being directly contrary to the teachings of Jesus and the early church fathers. Pelagius argued that God had given

---

[3] Maisie Ward, *Saint Jerome* (London: Sheed & Ward, 1950).

[4] Vulgate means "in the common tongue."

[5] Brinley Rees, ed., *Pelagius: Life and Letters* (Woodbridge: The Boydell Press, 1991).

a general grace to all mankind through Jesus Christ, but that he also gave instructions for living a godly life through the teachings of Moses and Jesus so that people might obtain this grace by righteous living. Moreover, man had been given the free will to be able to obey God's commandments and thereby to obtain the offered grace.

Because of his view of grace, Pelagius denied that original sin had destroyed man's ability to please God and to come to a saving faith on his own. Since people had what they needed to become morally upright children of God, Pelagius argued that the church was wrong in forgiving sins simply because people repented. After being scolded by other theologians, Pelagius left Rome and campaigned around the Mediterranean Basin, finding acceptance in some places but repudiation in others. Following his condemnation by the Council of Carthage in 418, he retreated to Egypt, where he died. Because he was regarded as a heretic, few of his writings survived.

Augustine of Hippo (354–430)[6] was a Berber, born in what is now Souk Ahras in Algeria. His mother, Monica, was a Christian, but his father was a pagan who joined the church only on his deathbed. Augustine's family was upper class, so he was well educated in Latin and classical studies. At age seventeen, he began an affair with a lower-class woman which lasted for fifteen years and produced a son named Adeodatus. About age twenty Augustine started a school of rhetoric in Carthage. Nine years later he moved his school to Rome. During this period, he joined the Manichaeans (see chapter 2), but he never progressed beyond the lowest level in their religious structure. In Rome he found political connections that led to his appointment in 384 as a rhetoric professor in Milan, the imperial western Roman capital.

While in Milan, Augustine went to hear Ambrose preach. Although he had never been impressed with Christianity, his time spent listening to Ambrose changed him and set him on a new course. Augustine converted to Christianity with his son in 386 and began his studies of church teachings. Two years later he returned to Africa. On the way his mother died and, soon afterward, also his son. At that point Augustine sold his family property and adopted the monastic lifestyle. In 391 he was ordained a priest, and in 395 he became bishop of Hippo Regius in what is now Algeria. Over the next thirty-five years he became the dominant churchman in the Latin-speaking world. He led the

---

[6]   Gerald Bonner, *St. Augustine of Hippo: Life and Controversies* (Philadelphia: The Westminister Press, 1963).

charge against his former religion, Manichaeism, as well as against Donatism (see chapter 3). He attacked the teachings of Pelagius and worked to get him removed from the Christian church. He was an ardent scholar. He is best known for *The Confessions of St Augustine*,[7] his autobiography, and *The City of God*,[8] which pointed people to the enduring kingdom of God rather than the changing empires of man. His theology became influential in both the Roman Catholic and the Protestant branches of the church. He died shortly before Hippo was overrun by the Vandals.

The Fall of Rome

The lands north of Italy had all been invaded by the beginning of the fifth century. Various Germanic tribes crossed the Alps and began menacing the Roman capital in Milan and then Ravenna. Under Alaric in 410, the Visigoths penetrated further southward and sacked Rome. It was a minor sacking, and the Visigoths quickly withdrew, but the damage to Roman pride was immense. By 418 the Romans had granted the Visigoths land in Gaul, but the deal did not last long. The Visigoths broke free of any loyalty to Rome and spread throughout southern Gaul, driving the Vandals, another Germanic tribe, into Hispania (modern Spain and Portugal).

The Vandals, Visigoths, Ostrogoths, Franks, and other Germanic tribes were being shoved west by the pressure of the Huns. The situation became even graver when Attila assumed the leadership of the Huns and drove against the Germanic tribes in Gaul and also against the Balkans and northern Italy. Attila bled ransom money from governors and emperors in return for not raiding their territories. Nevertheless, by 452 the Huns were on the verge of overrunning Italy. The pope begged Attila to stop. Then the unthinkable happened: Attila suddenly died, and his empire fell apart in the hands of his squabbling lieutenants.

In the power vacuum that developed after the collapse of the Huns, the Ostrogoths seized the Adriatic coastal areas and the land north of Italy. Meanwhile, the Roman government in the West was fighting losing battles on all fronts. Help from the eastern emperor and occasional minor successes could

---

7   William R. Cook and Ronald B. Herzman, *The Confessions of St Augustine* (Chantilly, Virginia: The Great Courses Teaching Company, 2004).

8   Charles Mathewes, *The City of God* (Chantilly, Virginia: The Great Courses Teaching Company, 2016).

not reverse the shrinking Roman power base and territorial control. On September 4, 476, soldiers loyal to Germanic leader Odoacer captured Rome. Although Odoacer nominally became the western emperor for sixteen years, the eastern emperor refused to recognize that the western empire had fallen and that Rome was, in reality, being ruled by a man of Germanic descent.

The Council of Ephesus (431)

While military chaos reigned in the western part of the empire, theological chaos had again come to the Greek-speaking East. The immediate cause was a dispute between **Nestorius**, Patriarch of Constantinople, and **Cyril**, Patriarch of Alexandria, over whether Mary should be referred to as "Christ bearer" or "God bearer." Nestorius asked Emperor Theodosius II to call an ecumenical church council to resolve the matter. In response, Theodosius called the Council of Ephesus,[9] which met in 431 at the Church of Mary. About 250 bishops came to consider the matter. Nestorius wanted to emphasize the difference between Christ's human and divine natures and wanted to change the terminology in common usage by the church at the time to do so. The root cause of the argument was that Nestorius believed that there could not be a union between Christ's human and divine natures. In effect, the two natures dwelled in one body, but they were not one person. The council condemned Nestorius's teaching and removed him from his position as Patriarch of Constantinople. Nestorius then fled east to Persia. The condemnation of his teachings caused what became known as the "Nestorian Schism," which still exists today. His teachings are held by the Assyrian Church of the East, the Ancient Church of the East, and several Chaldean churches. While initially large, these bodies shrank from the pressure of Islam.

The council was particularly contentious because the pope had already condemned Nestorius's teachings and sent representatives to insist that Nestorius be excommunicated. John, Patriarch of Antioch, showed up to defend Nestorius, but his delegation was not seated. The arguments by the Nestorian party were beaten back by a majority of the bishops. A clear decision was reached, which was gradually accepted in the eastern church as it had already been in the West, except by those previously mentioned. In addition, the council reaffirmed the Nicene Creed, requiring all bishops to adhere to it. It reject-

---

[9]   Percival, "The Council of Ephesus," *The Seven Ecumenical Councils*, 191–242.

ed Pelagianism[10] and also declared that amillennialism[11] was the only correct teaching. Patriarch Cyril drafted twelve anathemas[12] against the Nestorians, but his unfortunate choice of words in one of his statements would lead to the next schism.

The Council of Chalcedon (451)

After the Council of Ephesus, a theological struggle broke out between two parties. One claimed that Christ originally had two natures, a divine nature and a human nature, but that they had merged at the incarnation into one nature. These people were called "Monophysites." The orthodox party claimed that Christ continued to have two natures, but the two natures were united in one person. While this distinction might seem unimportant to the novice, it had deep significance. If the Monophysite position was accepted, then Christ really did not fulfil God's perfect law as a human. For twenty years members of both sides called regional councils, condemned each other's teachings as being heretical, and removed each other's adherents from their church positions. Emperor Theodosius II had come to side with the Monophysites and supported the decisions of their councils over the objections of Pope Leo I of Rome. In 450 Theodosius II died, and Marcian became emperor. He threw out the decisions of his predecessor and called another ecumenical council for the following year. The largest assembly ever, 520 bishops, mostly from the East, attended the Council of Chalcedon in 451.[13] As was his custom, the pope refused to attend, but he sent legates to offer a document that presented his position on the matter, which he considered conclusive.[14]

As was unfortunately usual for these councils, the Council of Chalcedon became a chaotic mess of charges and countercharges. The majority quickly decided that the historical teaching that Christ had two separate natures but that they were united in one person was correct. It adopted what is called the

---

[10] The central belief of Pelagianism was that man's ability to obey God's will and obtain heaven was not degraded by Adam's fall. When this teaching was rejected, others took up the cause, arguing that while man's ability had been degraded, it had not been extinguished. Man on his own could still keep God's will sufficiently to earn God's favor to the extent that God would then complete man's justification. This was called Semi-Pelagianism.

[11] Amillennialism is the denial that there will be an earthy thousand-year reign by Christ.

[12] An anathema is a formal declaration of theological error.

[13] Percival, "The Council of Chalcedon," *The Seven Ecumenical Councils*, 243–296.

[14] The pope had wanted the council held in Italy where he would have presided, but it was held next door to Constantinople to please the emperor.

"Chalcedonian Definition," effectively a creed stating this doctrine clearly. It removed and disciplined those who taught otherwise. The problem was that various theologians had used the same words differently, especially Cyril of Alexandria, and this had caused misunderstandings. Finally, the document from the Roman pope was accepted, with clarifications. Numerous details about the church's organization and operations were also addressed.

The Second Council of Constantinople (553)

Like most heresies, Monophysitism did not go away simply because it was condemned and because its leading proponents were defrocked. While the Sees of Rome, Constantinople and Antioch had accepted the verdict of Chalcedon, many in Egypt had rejected it, based on Cyril's,[15] the Patriarch of Alexandria, unclear statement at the Council of Ephesus. These rebels formed what became known as the "Oriental Orthodox" churches. Emperor Justinian called the Second Council of Constantinople[16] in 553 for the purpose of reaffirming the verdict of the Council of Chalcedon and condemning writings known as "the three chapters" which attempted to undermine that decision. It was presided over by Eutychius, Patriarch of Constantinople, with the support of the patriarchs of Antioch, Alexandria, and Jerusalem. As usual, the pope, though he was residing in Constantinople at the time due to the chaotic situation in Italy, refused to attend. The council moved quickly through its agenda, but the pope condemned its decision. The pope was therefore excommunicated and arrested with his advisors. Six months later he relented and accepted the decision, which oddly enough he had always favored. He just did not want to give any prestige to the other patriarchs by sitting with them because he believed he was their superior. With the verdict of this Second Council at Constantinople, the break with the Oriental Orthodox churches became permanent. Eventually, the latter churches were decimated by the advance of Islam.

The chaos in the remnants of the western empire

During the fifth century, the Visigoths took over much of Gaul, and they

---

[15] Cyril's statement can be misread to indicate that the two natures of Christ are merged within the one person.
[16] Percival, "The Second Council of Constantinople," *The Seven Ecumenical Councils*, 297–324.

also captured most of Hispania. The Vandals were shoved out of Hispania to the south and attacked and seized Roman territory in northern Africa. The western Roman armies ceased to be a force there. The struggle for control became one between the Vandals and the native Berbers. Only the Greek-speaking eastern section of North Africa remained under the control of the empire, that is, under the control of the emperor in Constantinople.

Meanwhile, further north, another change was occurring. The Franks, a powerful Germanic tribe, entered into Gaul and began pushing the Visigoths south. Under Clovis I in 507, the Franks defeated the Visigoths and drove them into Hispania. In 589 the Visigoths converted from Arian to Nicene Christianity. They ruled in Hispania and gradually became assimilated into the native population. During this period, the Frankish kingdoms gained control over the entire region of Gaul, except Burgundy, Provence, and Brittany. Because the Frankish rulers customarily divided their kingdoms among all their sons, the Franks were unable to take advantage of their superior numbers to establish a unified state in Gaul during the sixth century. The struggle for control of the sections of Gaul among Frankish groups and between the Franks and other Germanic tribes destroyed much of the remnants of Roman civil life. North of the Alps the instruments of Roman civilization were gradually trashed, pushing the inhabitants into a far more primitive lifestyle than they had known under the Romans.

In Italy it was hard to tell the players even with a scorecard! The Germanic Ostrogoths under Theodoric invaded Italy in 493 and killed Odoacer, the Germanic leader who had captured Rome in 476. With Theodoric came perhaps 200,000 of his subjects. This new kingdom of the Ostrogoths included Italy, Sicily, Switzerland, Slovenia, and beyond until 552. Their rule, however, was not unchallenged. The emperor of the eastern part of the former Roman Empire, henceforth called the Byzantine Empire,[17] launched attacks against the Vandals in North Africa and then against the Ostrogoths in northern Italy. Finally, Byzantine troops defeated the Ostrogoths in 552, and these foreigners were assimilated into the Italian population. It was a hollow and short-lived victory. The destruction to the fabric of Italian society had been horrendous during this period of warfare. That destruction continued with the invasion by another Germanic tribe, the Lombards, in 568. For almost forty years the

---

[17] "Byzantine" was a name manufactured by historians. The people of the Eastern empire always called themselves "Romans."

Lombards fought the Byzantines and each other for control of Italian territory. When the fighting stopped in 605, Italy was divided into numerous independent regions. It no longer had any aura of Roman civilization.

Roman rule in Britain began to fall apart near the end of the fourth century when Rome had to withdraw most of its troops to defend Italy. The Celts from Scotland swept southward, trying to regain territory lost long before. The people in the south seemed to forget the skills they had learned under the Romans. Buildings and roads fell into needless decay. Meanwhile, Saxons who had once been mercenaries in the Roman legions, returned from the continent to raid the British coast or, with their families, to settle in the British countryside. Britain became divided into numerous states which frequently changed their names and their boundaries. Although Britain was nominally Christian, the lack of central authority led to a significant growth in paganism and barbarism.

By the end of the sixth century, life in western Europe had fallen far from the high point of Roman civilization four centuries before. Much of the culture and learning of the Roman era had been progressively torn down and trampled into the mud of ignorance. Survival became the central issue for the common people. Meanwhile, those with swords and horses raided and warred to obtain what seldom were long-lasting gains. A societal decline had fallen across western Europe, and even the church struggled to survive and make sense of it all.

5

The Early Middle Ages

AD 600–1000

By the beginning of the seventh century, things were a mess in western Europe, while in the east the Byzantines were continually warring against the latest reincarnation of the Persian Empire. The western Germanic tribes had come to accept orthodox Christianity, but the nature of Christianity was very local because the election/appointment of bishops was a local affair. Regional church councils met, but they had little power to compel conformity. The number of monks and monastic orders grew slowly as intelligent men wanted to be free of the increasingly backward and dangerous secular society. Little did the Christian world realize it was about to be facing a force far more fearful than pagan Rome.[1]

For clarity from this point, the Latin-speaking churches will be referred to as "Catholic" and the Greek-speaking churches as "Orthodox." Both branches of the church regarded themselves as "universal," "orthodox," and "catholic," but the uppercase terms will be used to reduce confusion between them.

---

[1] Engelbrecht, *Church History*, 90–157.

 Schaff, *History of the Christian Church*, Vol. 4.

 Aland, *A History of Christianity*, Vol. 1, 215–275.

 Philip Daileader, *The Early Middle Ages* (Chantilly, Virginia: The Great Courses Teaching Company, 2004).

 Dorsey Armstrong, *The Medieval World* (Chantilly, Virginia: The Great Courses Teaching Company, 2009), Lect. 1–13.

Islam

Muhammad (570–632)[2] lived in Mecca and was illiterate, but he married a wealthy widow and participated in her caravan trading business. The Arabian peninsula at the time was occupied by hundreds of warring tribes, and these tribes worshiped many gods who dwelled in the Kaaba.[3] Muhammad listened to the teachings of the local Jews and was impressed that they had a book that supposedly came from the one and only God. On his travels he also encountered heretical Christian groups that had not accepted the decisions of the ecumenical councils and, consequently, had incorrect teachings about Christ. Because he could not read, he was unable to study what the orthodox Christian church taught, and so he assumed those he met accurately presented Christian beliefs. Christians also had a book, like the Jews, and Muhammad was impressed both by the monotheism that Jews and Christians taught and by the fact that their faith was anchored in a firm source. To him, they were "the people of the book." Muhammad longed to convert his fellow Arabs to monotheism and give them their own book.

In 610 Muhammad claimed to have been visited by the angel Gabriel and commissioned as a prophet of the "one true god." He called the god who had sent Gabriel to him "Allah"[4] and designated himself as the "Prophet of Allah." For years, few people paid attention to him, and many resented him because Mecca, with the Kaaba, greatly profited from the visitors who came to worship there. Under local pressure, Muhammad fled to Medina in 622, where he found greater success. Although he had to support himself as a caravan raider for a time, he gradually attracted enough followers to gain control of Medina, then to dominate the surrounding area, and finally to capture Mecca in 630. He cleansed the Kaaba of all its idols and declared it the holy ground of Islam.[5] Muhammad died two years later. Many who initially joined him in his battles were not believers in Islam, but they were in it for the plunder which they could get.

Muhammad began making prophetic statements, which are called "suras," in 610. He continued to make them throughout his life. At first, these suras

---

[2] Tor Andrae, *Mohammed: The Man and His Faith*, trans. Theophil Manzel (Mineola, New York: Dover Publications, 2000).

[3] The Kaaba was originally a holy building in Mecca filled with many gods. Pilgrims from the various Arab tribes came to worship these gods.

[4] "Allah" is the Arabic version of "El," which is a proper Hebrew name for "God."

[5] The word "Islam" itself means "submission."

were very mild, promoting monotheism. Some of the later suras were more emphatic and even militant. A few ran hundreds of lines, while others were only a few lines. Because he could not write, his followers had to memorize the suras, and some made their own written copies of them. The suras were not collected until after Muhammad's death to form the holy book of Islam, the Qur'an,[6] the title of which means "recite." They were not organized into the order in which they were spoken, which sometimes makes it difficult to determine the historical context of the suras. Faithful Muslims learn to recite all or large portions of the Qur'an.

The Spread of Islam

After Muhammad's death the leadership of Islam fell to Abu Bakr and, after his death, to Umar ibn al-Khattab.[7] Within five years, Muslim armies defeated both the Byzantine Empire and the Sassanid Empire, based in Persia, and took much land from each. What is now Syria, Palestine, Lebanon, and Iraq were overrun. The formerly great empires were driven back because they had exhausted themselves fighting each other. The Muslims conquered the remainder of the Sassanid Empire in 651. Their push westward across North Africa continued until the Atlantic Ocean was reached by 700. Almost all the people living in countries overrun by Muslims were gradually converted to Islam, sometimes by force, but more often by extra taxation or by social pressure to conform. The conquest of the Middle East and Northern Africa dealt a crushing blow to eastern Christianity, because it lost all its patriarchies, except Constantinople.

In 711 the Muslim general Tariq ibn-Ziyad attacked Hispania and overthrew the Visigoths who had been reigning there since the fifth century. He consolidated his control over most of the peninsula. All or part of Hispania remained under Muslim rule until near the end of the fifteenth century. From Hispania, the Muslims crossed the Pyrenees and advanced into France. At the battle of Tours in 732, they were defeated by the Frankish leader **Charles Martel** and gradually driven back into Hispania. Divisions in the Muslim

---

[6] Usama K. Dakdok, *The Generous Qur'an* (Venice, Florida: Usama Dakdok Publishing, LLC, 2009).

[7] Eamonn Gearon, *Turning Points in Middle Eastern History* (Chantilly, Virginia: The Great Courses Teaching Company, 2016), Lect. 1–12.

world undercut further advances into Europe in the west, although they did gradually overrun Sicily.

The Third Council of Constantinople (680–681)

Although its provinces were being overrun by the Muslims, the Byzantine Empire and the Orthodox church were still struggling over whether Christ had two natures but only one "energy" (Monoenergism) or two natures with separate energies and over whether he had one will (Monothelitism) or two wills. The fifth ecumenical council had supposedly decided these issues, but in Palestine, Syria, and Egypt the controversy would not die. Perhaps the only reason the one-nature and one-will side did not prevail, at least in the Orthodox churches, was because so many Christians in the eastern provinces converted to Islam, undermining the strength of the churches there. The popes came out solidly against both Monothelitism and Monoenergism, so the issues had basically become moot in the Catholic Church. Only thirty-seven bishops met for this "ecumenical" council in Constantinople, with the Byzantine emperor presiding at some of the sessions.[8] The council decided against the one-nature and one-will positions. As usual, opposing bishops were deposed.

Disarray Across "Christian" Europe

Perhaps what made the Early Middle Ages particularly dark during the seventh century was that nothing of significance was happening in Europe. The Franks were haphazardly consolidating their power in Gaul, thereby giving it the name by which it would henceforth be known, "France."[9] The Franks also tried to dominate the Germanic tribes farther to the east, such as the Saxons, but these tribes resisted because they were also being pressured by the Slavic tribes from their east and could not retreat.

The papal control over the church was quite limited, with local bishops and abbots free to do as they pleased as long as they had enough political and financial support to maintain their independence. In Ireland monks became more prominent in society, while in England all thing Romans were in decline. Some Irish monks came to the continent as missionaries to the tribes still in Germany or to instill better virtue into the nominally Christian Franks.

---

[8]　Percival, "The Third Council of Constantinople," *The Seven Ecumenical Councils*, 325–354.

[9]　In Germany today France is still called *Frankreich*, the kingdom of the Franks.

It was in the area of learning and language that the gloom of the Early Middle Ages was most apparent. In Roman times, Latin was spoken as a common language across the western empire, and almost everyone could understand it. It was a necessity for conducting business both as the seller or as the buyer. Moreover, many people could read, at least at a basic level. By the seventh century neither of these conditions was true. The members from various Germanic tribes that had entered the former empire brought their own languages. These became blended with the local languages and Latin. Simultaneously, travel diminished as the Roman roads deteriorated and as bandits multiplied. Western Europe gradually became a large collection of semi-isolated areas speaking their own dialects. Only in the Catholic Church was Latin retained as the means of universal communication, although secular rulers often had Latin-speaking scribes and lawyers to conduct their official business. Even in the church, however, the level of education of the parish priests declined, becoming far lower than it had been in earlier times because the priests came primarily from the illiterate lower classes. The use of religious symbols and rituals increased as a method of communication with the bulk of the church members who could no longer understand the Latin words used by the churchmen. The principle of *ex opere operato*[10] progressively became an accepted teaching of the Catholic Church.

One more issue deeply troubled the church. Since its earliest days, there had been a strong push for the clergy to be celibate. Many church leaders over the years had adopted this lifestyle to facilitate carrying out their calls. Nevertheless, with the large influx of people into the Christian church subsequent to Christianity becoming the state religion in 394, the number of men who were willing to become priests if they had to remain celibate was far fewer than the number of priests needed. To address the shortage, numerous married men from the lower classes were allowed to enter the clergy, but a distinction was made between them and those who chose what was regarded as the more noble path of celibacy. The members of the former group were called the "secular clergy"[11] to distinguish them from the "regular clergy" who vowed not to marry. The secular clergy were usually poorly trained, and in a society where crime was rampant, they often behaved little differently than the mem-

---

[10] *Ex opere operato* means getting the religious benefit of an action merely by doing it without having to understand or believe it.

[11] The actual term "secular clergy" did not come into use until sometime later, but it is used here to correctly reflect the nature of those who were not "regular clergy."

bers of the communities they served. It was during this period that "penance" in place of "penitence" began to be the dominant teaching in many parishes. Everyone, including the priests, had to "pay off" their well-known public sins by doing assigned good works. To lure men into the "celibate" priesthood, many bishops allowed men who agreed not to marry to keep a concubine for an annual fee.[12] These priests were formally single for church purposes, but essentially married. Things were rotten, and the church survived by finding ways to use the Law as a curb for gross sins, even if it was not using it as an effective mirror for people to see their true condition before God.

The Sacramental System

From its earliest times, there were always "sacred acts" performed in the Christian church. These were acts administered by the clergy to bring the people closer to God by emphasizing God's love for them. These acts were solemn actions due to their perceived holiness. Certainly, Holy Baptism was always considered a sacred act because it had been commanded by Jesus. In the same way, Holy Communion was regarded as a sacred act because Jesus instituted it. Which other acts were regarded as "sacred" varied from place to place because the Bible did not give a list of rites which the church was to perform. As Europe entered the darkness of the Early Middle Ages, particularly in the West, sacred acts became more important in communicating God's love to a progressively uneducated laity.

Church leaders saw the necessity of keeping control over the proliferation of the sacred acts, so they gave special status to some acts by calling them "sacraments." These sacraments were regarded as having been authorized by God in some manner. The best way to maintain control of the sacraments was to restrict their administration to the clergy. To do this, the church made the act of becoming a clergyman one of the sacraments, later called "Holy Orders," that only bishops could perform. This closed the system to the laity. Baptism and Holy Communion were always universally regarded as sacraments. Marriage gained recognition as a sacrament in an effort to wrest control of it from the state when the Roman Empire Christianized and subse-

---

[12] This was technically a type of penance for those who could not keep the vow of celibacy, because such an arrangement was only regarded as a venial sin, which required only temporal punishment.

quently collapsed in the West. Penance was also raised to the status of a sacrament for reasons stated in the previous section.

Determining which sacred acts were to be considered sacraments was not done in a systematic fashion. It differed across the church. In the West "confirmation" came to be regarded as a sacrament, while in the East, "christening" was held to be a sacrament. The number of sacraments therefore differed among regions of the church for centuries. It was finally set as seven in the West by the Council of Florence in 1439, which added to the list what at the time was called the "Last Rites," but which is now called the "Anointing of the Sick." No such formal declaration was made in the Orthodox churches. As years passed, the sacramental system became of critical importance in the Roman Catholic Church as a means to earn merit toward salvation.

The Second Council of Nicaea (787)

Beginning already in the first century, those who had been put to death because of their faith (i.e., the martyrs) had been honored by others in the church. People would gather at their graves to remember them on the anniversaries of their death. Unfortunately, over the years, at least in some places, such honors resulted in establishing shrines to the martyrs. In addition, some who had worshiped a pantheon of gods in their previous religion came into Christianity predisposed to seeking help for the various aspects of life from gods identified with those aspects. Christian leaders found it convenient to encourage such people to turn instead to the examples of specific Christians of the past as models of how God helped them in their trials. These people soon began to venerate these "saints" and even seek their active intervention as they had done with the pagan deities, e.g., St. Joseph for carpentry. Saint worship progressively became a part of the church's practice, at least informally. As it spread, some in the church pushed to organize it for "the benefit of the souls of the common people," while others opposed it as heresy. In the eighth century, the issue came to a head when Byzantine Emperor Constantine V banned the veneration of icons,[13] initiating what has come to be called the Iconoclastic Controversy.

While Constantine V had been supported by the regional Council of Hieria, the matter became a hot issue throughout the whole Christian Church. Con-

---

[13] An icon is most commonly a painted image of a saint or Jesus.

stantine and his son, Leo IV, vigorously enforced the ban through the persecution of dissenters. After Leo's death, his widow, acting as regent for their son, began making changes in the governmental policy and the church leadership. The Second Council of Nicaea[14] was called in 787 to review the issue after iconoclast supporters disrupted the first attempt to hold an assembly in Constantinople. At this council, icons and religious art were brought back. Veneration, but not worship, of icons and other religious artwork was permitted and encouraged. It was claimed that veneration of these objects was veneration of those whom they represented. The council also decreed that each altar should contain a relic of a saint. With this decision, the Christian church formally went beyond using icons for education to using them to practice idolatry. The Frankish clergy, however, rejected both the banning and worshiping of icons, restricting them to educational and inspirational purposes. Therefore, this is an appropriate time to look at the realm of the Franks.

The Merovingian Kingdom (481–751)

The Merovingians were a Frankish family that gained political strength at the beginning of the sixth century. In northern France, the Merovingians had closely associated themselves with the remnants of the Roman power structure and took over as it collapsed. King Clovis I, a convert to "catholic" Christianity, united numerous other Frankish tribes and gradually gained at least nominal control over most of France. His sons continued to expand the realm, but because they each divided their land holdings among all their sons, there was a continual struggle for power within the family. In 613 Chlothar II reunited the Merovingians into a single kingdom that lasted until 687. After that date the realm was again divided, with the head stewards (called "mayors of the palace") of the regional rulers often exercising more power than their Merovingian princes. The Merovingians were a good example of why society did not evolve in western Europe during this period. The rulers were too much committed to their own petty interests rather than to the welfare of the people they ruled. The peasants, on the other hand, hoped the rulers would just ignore them.

---

[14] Percival, "The Second Council of Nice," *The Seven Ecumenical Councils*, 521–588.

The Carolingian Empire (751–843)

Charles Martel[15] (688–741) was a duke and prince of the Franks whose family had become mayors of the palace for the king and for other key leaders. Charles was not the designated heir to the power of the Carolingian family and was imprisoned to prevent him from gaining power. He escaped confinement during one of the numerous civil wars among the Merovingians and began gathering his own army. By 723 he had defeated his rivals and had become mayor of the palace under the Merovingian king. He continued to expand his power by constant warfare in Germany against the Saxons and other tribes until he controlled the western half of Germany. In 732 he defeated a Muslim army at Tours. He spent the rest of his life subduing Burgundy and southwestern France. Charles created the system of interlocking alliances that became known as feudalism (see chapter 7).

In 737 the Merovingian king Theodoric IV died, and no one was strong enough to take the throne without Charles's support. The throne remained vacant. Meanwhile, Charles's lands were divided among his sons after his death in 741. Pepin the Short emerged as the sole ruler after his brother opted for the religious life and after Pepin defeated his half-brother in battle. By 747 Pepin controlled the power of France, and in 751, with the support of Pope Zachary, he ousted the last Merovingian king and declared himself king of the Frankish domains. He battled continually to shove back the Saxons and the Bavarians, but he failed to gain complete dominance. At his death in 768, he divided his kingdom between his sons Carloman and Charlemagne.

As usual, there was a struggle between the brothers, but it ended with the convenient death of Carloman at the end of 771. Meanwhile, Charlemagne had strengthened his position by marrying the daughter of the king of the Lombards who ruled northern Italy. He himself became king of the Lombards in 774. He defeated the Germanic tribes as far as the Elbe River and forcibly converted them to Christianity. The Carolingians came to see the importance of religious unity in their kingdom, and therefore they forged a close relationship with the papal office. The popes gave tacit approval to Charlemagne's concubines and his naked aggression in Germany, while they provided him with protection from and influence over other church leaders in his realm.[16]

---

[15]   Martel means "the hammer."

[16]   The papacy was trapped between two things that it dearly wanted. On one hand, the papacy wanted to manage the secular affairs of Europe, which required powerful rulers who had

Moreover, there had been a long fiction that the Roman Empire still existed in its entirety, with the Byzantine emperors still appointing rulers in Italy as their adjuncts in the West. On Christmas Day 800, the pope demolished this fiction by crowning Charlemagne the "Roman Emperor," thereby giving western Europe an emperor independent of the Byzantines. Thus was founded the interesting and often absurd entity called the Holy Roman Empire, which lasted until it was destroyed by Napoleon I in 1806.

Charlemagne lived until 814. At his death the Frankish kingdom controlled all of modern France, Austria, northern Italy, most of Germany, and even some lands to the east. Charlemagne's successor was his only surviving son, Louis the Pious. Louis made the mistake of trying to divide his empire into three kingships for his eldest sons while he was still living, which led to multi-sided civil wars that continued to 843. The Treaty of Verdun in that year divided Frankish lands into a western, a central, and an eastern portion, which has shaped Europe ever since. It produced a temporary truce, but struggles continued as family members died or showed themselves to be ineffective rulers. The problem of rulers dividing their lands among their sons further contributed to the growing chaos in the Carolingian lands. In 888 the Frankish kingdom was permanently divided among the family members, and only the myth of a united Europe remained.

The Appearance of the Vikings

If the Franks and all western Europe feared the growth of Islam to their south in the eighth century, they were soon to face another peril to their north. That peril proved even more difficult for them to deal with militarily. Beginning in the 790s, the Vikings,[17] also known as Norsemen, began raiding the British Isles and continental Europe from Brittany to the Volga River. They had boats that could sail the North Sea and the Baltic Sea, but they could also sail the Atlantic Ocean. In addition, these ships could be sailed many miles

---

obligations to the popes. Unfortunately, such rulers often also had a lust for women. On the other hand, the papacy needed to insist that marriage was a less honorable spiritual estate than celibacy to keep its clergy in line. It could not legitimize concubinary, as in the Old Testament, without giving legal status to the concubines of priests. It therefore degraded marriage to the point where there was little spiritual distinction in having a wife, concubines, or mistresses, all being merely different degrees of venial sin. The ghosts of the second century would not go away.

17 Kenneth W. Harl, *The Vikings* (Chantilly, Virginia: The Great Courses Teaching Company, 2005), Lect. 1–16.

up rivers into the heartlands of nations. The Vikings were Scandinavian, and they were pagan. They had little respect for life and none for Christianity. They plundered and destroyed villages and monasteries indiscriminately. They kidnapped lords for ransom and peasants to sell elsewhere as slaves.

The Vikings attacked where they pleased, but during this period it was their attacks on Britain and northern France that were most disturbing. While England and Scotland saw their share of warfare as did the continent, a great monastic tradition arose in them as well. It was led by scholars such as the Venerable Bede and Alcuin of York. This growth in monasticism led to the building of large monasteries that acquired both literary and monetary wealth. The Vikings cared little for the former, but they were extremely interested in the latter. Most of the monasteries were built close to the seacoast or on navigable rivers. They were, therefore, easy targets for the Viking raiders. During the entire ninth century, Vikings were a regular peril to the coastal communities, and by the middle of the ninth century, they began to attack farther inland. The English rulers were unable to prevail against the Vikings, who at this point were mostly Danish, and began to pay them "danegeld" to buy them off. The Vikings, however, continued to press into the middle of England, determined to dominate the whole country. They were finally stopped by the king of Wessex, but the Danes still controlled the eastern side of England. They began bringing over their families to strengthen their hold on the territory that they had overrun. They also began to convert to Christianity.

Viking attacks against the northern coast of France also started about the beginning of the ninth century. Charlemagne's mighty army was not prepared to deal with this type of hit-and-run attack from the sea. The situation only got worse as subsequent Frankish rulers wasted their strength fighting each other. Unlike England, the wealth of France was not on its coasts, so the initial Viking raids were more of a nuisance than a threat to the control of the country as they were in England. As time passed, however, the Vikings began coming up the French rivers and raiding places well inland. There was no good defense. The Vikings could move too quickly by water to be threatened by a land army. If the army was on one side of the river, the Vikings would attack on the other. Finally, in 911 the French king ceded the area that would become known as Normandy, "the land of the Norse," to a strong Viking group. In return for the land, these Vikings became vassals of the king of France and agreed to help defend France. By convincing these raiders to become settlers, the Franks could continue their favorite pastime of fighting each other.

The political situation across Europe and England remained unsettled for many centuries. Before we consider it further, however, we need to return to the religious realm. Another power struggle was occurring which would greatly impact the development of Western Christianity. This struggle involved the efforts of the papacy to gain absolute religious control of the Christian church, as well as political control of all temporal rulers. Our detour to consider this situation will help our understanding of what went before and of what came after this point in the history of Christianity in Europe.

6

The Growth of the Papacy

The "Bishop of Rome," the "pope," the "holy father," "Christ's vicar on earth," the "Great Antichrist" – call its occupant what you will, the papacy is one of the strangest institutions that has ever existed. It has been religious. It has been secular. It has been demonic! Now that we have looked at how the secular and religious worlds developed for nine hundred years, it is time to review the development of the papacy, as it is necessary for understanding the next stages in European history.[1]

Early Roots

The church at Rome might be said to have begun on the first Pentecost because people from Rome were among those converted by the Holy Spirit when Peter preached the first sermon of the Christian church.[2] Certainly, this gave Peter a connection to Rome, but it might have been his only connection.

---

[1] Thomas F. X. Noble, *Popes and the Papacy: A History* (Chantilly, Virginia: The Great Courses Teaching Company, 2006).

Engelbrecht, *Church History*, 90–157.

Schaff, *History of the Christian Church*, Vols. 4, 5.

Aland, *A History of Christianity*, Vol. 1, 215–413.

Daileader, *The Early Middle Ages*.

Philip Daileader, *The High Middle Ages*, (Chantilly, Virginia: The Great Courses Teaching Company, 2001).

Armstrong, *The Medieval World*, Lect. 17–20.

[2] "...visitors from Rome, both Jews and proselytes...." (Acts 2:10)

The church in Rome was very fluid in its early days, both due to the many comings to and goings from the eternal city and because it was the capital of the empire and a center of trade. Moreover, periodically Jews and Christians had to flee the city due to imperial edicts or persecution. In its own self-image, Rome was a city of legends. Romans were supposedly descended from Aeneas and his band of warriors who had escaped Troy when it was destroyed.[3] Rome had been, according to legend, founded by Romulus and Remis, twin boys raised by a wolf. In Rome having a pedigree was everything, and that Roman Christians created their own pedigree as being the "church of Peter," the leading apostle, was only natural.[4]

The exact order of bishops in Rome during the first century is unclear. About the end of the first century, Clement, a Roman bishop, wrote a letter to the church in Corinth. Rome, however, remained more of an outpost in the west for Christianity, which was centered in the eastern Mediterranean Basin. Myths about the role of Peter in Rome began to grow during this period, particularly alleged battles of magic between him and Simon the magician from Samaria.[5] Meanwhile, Christianity in the West spread into Gaul and northern Africa. In fact, with the appearance of Tertullian, Latin Christianity in northern Africa often overshadowed that in Rome through the time of Augustine. Even Ambrose in Milan was better known than most of the Roman bishops of the time.

Despite this, the citizens of Rome used their position at the nominal seat of governmental power[6] to argue that Rome was where Christ would have wanted his church headquartered. By the fourth century Rome had generally come to be regarded throughout Christendom as the "See of St. Peter." Despite this, it was only one of the four great patriarchies of the church, and it became one of five with the establishment of Constantinople as the capital of the empire. Indeed, the new patriarchy of Constantinople was well-positioned to assert itself because it was at the center of political power.

---

[3] Virgil, *The Aeneid*, trans. Johann Grüninger (Franklin Center, Pennsylvania: The Franklin Library, 1982).

[4] There is no biblical evidence that Peter ever went to Rome, and the claim that he spent time in Rome is difficult to reconcile with what is written in the Bible. Some suggest that he made it to Rome at the end of his life and was executed there. There is insufficient evidence to establish this. Extra-biblical references to Peter and Rome are of uncertain authenticity.

[5] *The Lost Books of the Bible.*

[6] The working capital had actually moved to Milan by this time. The popes took as much advantage as they could of the power vacuum to elevate their position in Rome.

Nevertheless, during the fourth century the Bishop of Rome was able to maintain his prestigious position due to the growing doctrinal divisions within the eastern church. Even such a prominent churchman as Athanasius, the Patriarch of Alexandria, needed to appeal to Rome to intervene on his behalf in his theological disputes. Rome was regarded as an objective ear concerning the hotly debated issues in the East. Moreover, the pope maintained his claim of superiority over the other patriarchs by never attending an ecumenical church council but only sending representatives. These representatives presented the papal position, which the pope expected to be accepted. He was not about to degrade himself by attending councils called by emperors, who, after all, were laymen.

Dealing with Unstable Times

In the fifth century the western Roman Empire grew more and more unstable as it lost lands to the various Germanic tribes. The western capital had not been in Rome for many years, which meant the pope did not have as much direct influence on the government as he liked to claim. Despite this, the Romans maintained that their bishop occupied the See of Peter and was therefore supreme in the church. In particular, Pope Leo I (400–461) worked to promote the doctrine of Petrine supremacy. To strengthen their leadership in the West, the popes needed to engage the mostly Arian Christians among the Germanic tribes. The papacy also had to deal with the power vacuum that occurred as the Roman government collapsed and as the Germanic leaders struggled for supremacy in Italy. The popes therefore tried to act as powerbrokers to enhance the position of the papacy and protect what they could of orthodox Christianity. Slowly, the representatives of the Roman church and its allies pushed the Arians out of the churches in Gaul and regained the territory north of the Alps. The popes cut whatever deals they could in the face of the violence that dominated the land. A major concern for the popes was the Arian Lombards in northern Italy who, of course, did not recognize papal authority.

An intermittent doctrinal, political, and sometimes personal struggle was fought between Constantinople (the "New Rome") and the old Rome. Each group eyed the other with suspicion and claimed to be the seat of Christianity. Various incidents sparked turmoil. For example, the immediate cause of the Acacian Schism in 484, in which Pope Felix III excommunicated Patriarch Acacius, was the toleration of Monophysitism in the Greek-speaking East.

Gregory I (540–604),[7] the great-grandson of Pope Felix III, was the first pope about whom much is known. Gregory was made prefect[8] of Rome by the Byzantine emperor in 572. He soon tired of the job and spent some time in a monastery, but he returned to public life as a representative to Constantinople. After returning to Rome, he was elected pope in 590. He managed to get many of the Germanic Arians to join the Catholic Church, greatly increasing papal influence in the West. He dominated Rome both politically and religiously. He sent missionaries to the Anglo-Saxons in Britain. He introduced Gregorian chant to the worship service.

By the beginning of the eighth century, religious issues were becoming divisive in the empire. Emperor Justinian II responded by calling his own council to deal with these issues, but Pope Sergius I (pope from 687–701) rejected the decisions of the council.[9] During this century there were constant religious and political struggles between the popes and the Byzantine emperors. The emperor wanted Italian tax money to finance the defense of the eastern empire, but he did not want to provide military forces to stabilize Italy. The emperors also wanted to end the use of icons in the church, as noted previously. The popes firmly opposed these two initiatives. Without Byzantine help against the Lombards, the popes grew desperate and appealed to the Franks. After some dawdling, the help came in 773 in the person of Charlemagne, who defeated the Lombards. He cut a territorial deal with the pope, giving to the pope the land which would become known as the Papal States. In 800 Pope Leo II crowned Charlemagne as emperor, thereby making a clean political break with the Byzantines.

Unfortunately for the papacy, Carolingian power in Italy soon began to decline. In 846 Muslim pirates sacked Catholic churches in Rome. The countryside became unsafe. Pope John VIII was brutally murdered in 882. Things became unglued in Rome. Murder, mayhem and mistresses dominated papal politics for the next eighty years. Marozia (890–937), a Roman noblewoman, became a dominant female presence in Rome, sleeping with, begetting, naming, and removing popes seemingly at will. Occasionally, she would actually marry. Some stability returned in 962 when pope John XII (a grandson of Marozia) cut a deal with German King Otto I for protection in exchange for trad-

---

[7] H. Homes Dudden, *The Life and Times of Gregory I, the Great* (Amazon for Kindle).
[8] A prefect was a civil official appointed to act in the stead of the emperor.
[9] Pope Sergius also redid the Latin liturgy.

ing privileges. Under German protection the popes gained Poland and Hungary for the Catholic Church. They restructured the monasteries. In 993 John XV canonized the first "saint" (Bishop Ulrich of Augsburg) on behalf of the whole church. Previous saints had only been canonized locally.

Manufactured History

When necessary, the Roman church found it advantageous to manufacture history. About the third century, the Roman church tried to strengthen its position in Christianity as the legitimate seat of the Christian church. Supposedly, Peter had written a letter to James in Jerusalem informing him that he had transferred his position as head of the church to Clement in Rome. James then purportedly wrote back acknowledging the transfer. The forger, however, misdated James's alleged letter as having been written in AD 65, three years after James's death!

The Donation of Constantine was a decree, supposedly written in 315, which gave control of the western part of the empire to the pope in perpetuity as a thank-you gift for curing Constantine of leprosy. Both the cure and the decree were probably created in the eighth century. At that time, the papacy was struggling to assert its independence from the Byzantines and its authority over the western church. The document was dragged out periodically to assert papal power over the secular rulers in western Europe when they became contentious. This was especially true in the thirteenth century. It was during this period that a picture of Constantine the Great handing the decree to Pope Sylvester I was painted to commemorate the occasion. In the fifteenth century Catholic scholars discovered numerous errors of fact and style in the document, thereby establishing it as a fraud.

The *Pseudo–Isidorian Decretals,* written around 845, were a complete fabrication of church history. They described precedents for the exercising of papal authority over the whole Christian church prior to the fourth century. In them it appears that the popes had from the earliest times exercised sovereign dominion over the whole church, including ultimate authority over the seven ecumenical councils of the church.

The forgery mill continued working during subsequent years. A Latin forger created a large number of manufactured quotations allegedly taken from the works of the Greek church fathers such as Cyril of Jerusalem, John Chrysostom, and Cyril of Alexandria. He interspersed these with some genuine quotations to create the *Thesaurus of Greek Fathers*. To these quotes he added spurious canons from the early ecumenical councils. Pope Urban IV submitted this forgery to Thomas Aquinas, who, believing the quotes to be real, wrote his work *Against the Errors of the Greeks in the Defense of the Papacy*.

The forgery of relics began with Helena, Constantine's mother. Locals in Palestine duped her into believing they could supply her with the "true cross" and the nails that held Jesus on it. Others joined the lucrative manufacturing effort, particularly at the time of the crusades, when anything that allegedly came from Palestine brought a good price. This manufacture of "sacred relics" continued until the time of Luther and into modern history.

The Great Schism

The languages of the original Christian church were Greek and Aramaic. As the percentage of Christians in the church who spoke Greek grew, it became the dominant language throughout the church, even in Rome. In Italy outside of Rome and in northern Africa, however, the number of Latin-speaking Christians increased steadily. By the end of the second century, the church in Rome had also switched to Latin, and Latin began to dominate in the western churches. Switching languages can also induce changes in attitude. The Romans were better known as builders; the Greeks better known as philosophers.

The shift in political power further complicated the relations between the eastern and western churches. The Roman pope had insisted that he was the senior church leader when the Roman capital was in Rome, but the Patriarch of Constantinople began to assert his role when the capital moved to the eastern empire. Constantinople's position was further strengthened when the Sees of the other eastern patriarchies fell into Muslim hands. The Patriarch of Constantinople began to consider himself at least the equal of the Bishop of Rome.

Politics aside, theological differences had also developed between the eastern and western branches of the church. The eastern church claimed that the Holy Spirit proceeded only from the Father, but the western church claimed that he proceeded from both the Father and the Son. The use of leavened or unleavened bread in the Lord's Supper became an issue. Other issues involved liturgical rites and who could call and sit in a church council. In 1053 the pope decided to assert his authority and directed the Greek churches in southern Italy either to close or to adopt Latin practices. In response, the Patriarch of

Constantinople ordered the closure of all Latin churches in Constantinople. In 1054 Pope Leo IX sent a legate to Constantinople to inform the patriarch that his actions were unacceptable because the pope was the head of the whole church. The legate also asked the Byzantine Emperor for aid against the Normans who had invaded southern Italy. Patriarch Cerularius refused the demands of the pope, so Cardinal Humbert, the head of the papal delegation, excommunicated him. The patriarch responded by excommunicating the members of the delegation. In the meantime, Pope Leo had died, and his successor, Victor II, was not about to challenge the actions of the legate, which might have appeared to reduce his power. The split between the eastern and western churches was complete.

Hildebrand

The great consolidation of papal power in the eleventh century can be attributed in large part to a man often called Hildebrand (1015–1085),[10] who was named Lidebrando di Soana at birth and who died as Pope Gregory VII. Although from the lower classes, he was sent as a youth to the monastery of St. Mary on the Aventine. He became chaplain to Johannes Gratianus, who was chosen to be Pope Gregory VI in 1045. Unfortunately, three men claimed to be pope. Emperor Henry III of Germany intervened, threw out all three popes, and installed the Bishop of Bamberg as Pope Clement II. Gratianus fled to Cologne, and Hildebrand followed him there. After Gratianus's death in 1048, Hildebrand moved to Cluny, where he became a monk. Hildebrand, however, was not through with papal politics.

Hildebrand accompanied Abbot Bruno of Toul to Rome, where the latter was chosen in 1049 to be Pope Leo IX, under whom the Great Schism occurred . The new pope named Hildebrand as a deacon and papal administrator. Hildebrand was back in a powerful position, and he was sent as a papal legate to settle a controversy in Tours, France. After Leo's death in 1054, the next pope, Victor II, reaffirmed Hildebrand as legate. The new pope died in 1057. Next it was Stephen IX's turn on the papal throne, but he died the next year in Florence. With Hildebrand off on a mission to Germany, things fell apart in Rome. The Roman people, long accustomed to choosing one of their own favorites, were manipulated by the Roman aristocracy into selecting a new

---

[10]   H. E. J. Cowdrey, *Pope Gregory VII, 1073–1085* (Oxford: Clarendon Press, 1998).

pope who took the name Benedict X and who was the brother of one of the popes deposed by Henry III. When Hildebrand returned, he personally led three hundred knights to storm the castle where Benedict X was hiding and deposed him. Thereafter, Nicholas II assumed the papal throne but only held it for two years.

During Nicholas II's short reign, however, Hildebrand was made arch-deacon of the Roman church, the position that held the real power behind the papal throne. Under his leadership Nicholas restricted papal electors to those designated "cardinal bishops." In theory at least, the days of the election of the pope by mob rule or through appointment by the Holy Roman Emperor were over. In 1061 the papal vacancy was filled in the prescribed fashion by Pope Alexander III. He retained Hildebrand as his political operative. Under Hildebrand's leadership, a program of papal reform strengthened the office, and deals with local rulers were cut that gave the pope some protection against the German princes who had come to dominate the office of the Holy Roman Emperor.

After the death of Alexander, there was a popular outcry in Rome to make Hildebrand pope. Knowing this would undermine the election of future popes, Hildebrand fled and went into seclusion. When he was finally found hiding in a monastery, the cardinals made him pope by acclamation. The man who had been the power behind the popes suddenly was the pope, and he took the name Gregory VII in honor of the first pope he had served. Strangely, Hildebrand first had to be ordained as a priest and then consecrated as a bishop before he could become pope. He had been a church politician, not a religious leader. As pope, Gregory VII worked industriously to assert papal authority over the secular princes. He was in a constant struggle with Holy Roman Emperor Henry IV, whom he thrice excommunicated. He tried to play the Normans in the south of Italy off against the Germans, but the people of Rome did not take kindly to the overbearing Normans. In 1085, the year of his death, Gregory VII was forced to flee Rome for the Italian coast.

The Crusades

The Muslims had overrun Palestine in the seventh century, and they continued to attack the borders of the Byzantine Empire. In 1095 the Byzantine emperor requested military support from the western Christians to defend his territory. Pope Urban II saw this not only as an opportunity to save Christian lands from the Muslims but also as an opportunity to assert his control over the eastern church. In addition, he wanted to stop the infighting among Christians in Europe, which we will study in the next chapter. At the Council of Clermont, he called for a crusade to liberate the Holy Lands from Muslim rule.[11] He offered a plenary indulgence for anyone who joined the crusade.[12]

Attracted by the supposed offer of the complete forgiveness of their sins, many poorer people followed Peter the Hermit on a mob march across Europe to Constantinople. Along the way they killed Jews and extorted supplies from the Christians through whose lands they traveled. After they passed Constantinople, they were massacred by the Turks. A separate military group under the leadership of some of Europe's high nobility also proceeded by land to Constantinople. This group of perhaps 100,000 then continued their march into Muslim territory. Progress was slow, and casualties were heavy, often the result of inadequate supplies. The crusaders had to learn new methods of warfare to fight in the conditions that existed in Syria. Eventually, they captured Antioch and withstood a Muslim counterattack. They then proceeded to Jerusalem, which they captured. Unfortunately, along the way they had senselessly killed many civilians – Muslims, Jews, and Christians alike. The inhabitants of Jerusalem were likewise massacred. With Jerusalem in crusader hands, the rest of the Christian horde returned to Europe, except for three hundred knights and two thousand infantry. Those remaining established several small crusader states.

With the decrease in the crusader forces, it was only a few decades before the Muslims began to push back the crusader gains. Most important was the loss of Edessa to the Muslims in 1144. Two years later Pope Eugenius III called for a second crusade. The results of this crusade were very limited because the Christian rulers could not agree on their objectives and did not bring enough men to make permanent gains. Meanwhile in Europe, this call for another crusade caused numerous massacres of Jews and a new zeal for Christians to drive the Muslims out of Hispania.

---

[11]   Gearon, *Turning Points*, Lect. 14–16.
[12]   Indulgences had been in use for some time before the crusades. A plenary indulgence granted release from all temporal punishment imposed by the church for sins. This allowed people to avoid purgatory, and many believed it forgave their sins so they could enter heaven. A crusader had to confess and be absolved prior to taking the "crusader vow," but there was no subsequent requirement for confession and penance.

Struggles among the Muslims led to the rise of Saladin. He gained control over the Muslim Middle East from the Nile to the Euphrates. He recaptured Jerusalem and drove the crusaders to the sea. In 1189 Pope Gregory VIII called for the Third Crusade. The leading kings of Europe arrived with their armies, and they regained some of the territory that had been lost. They, however, had not brought enough resources to capture and hold Jerusalem, so they retired, leaving only a few crusader states along the Mediterranean Sea.

In 1198 Pope Innocent III launched the Fourth Crusade. The number of soldiers, 35,000, was impressive, but the travel arrangements became a nightmare. The Venetians demanded large sums of money to transport the crusaders. When they landed in the Byzantine Empire, the crusaders sacked Constantinople rather than moving south against the Muslims in Palestine. This crusade accomplished nothing except to weaken the already strained relations between the eastern and western churches. While other minor crusading efforts followed under subsequent popes, the recapturing of the Holy Lands no longer interested European leaders. Financing for the crusades was a constant problem, causing the popes to offer the same indulgence to those who contributed money to support the crusades as to those who went to fight. This decreased the desire of people to risk their lives on a crusade, hoping that they could buy their way into heaven with appropriate financial contributions.

A romantic legacy of the crusades is the orders of knights that they spawned. There were the Templars, the Hospitallers (also called the Knights of St John and Knights of Malta) and the Teutonic Knights. These groups were often based on nationality. They were monks as well as knights and were originally organized to protect pilgrims as they journeyed through Palestine to the holy sites of Christendom. They eventually became a major nuisance to European rulers who had no desire to have large groups of armed men meandering around in their countries once they returned from Palestine.

By the High Middle Ages, the papacy had become seriously corrupted by its desire to rule the Christian world. It permitted and sanctioned lying, stealing, murder, rebellion, simony,[13] and sexual sins when these furthered the goals of the Bishop of Rome. While there were faithful believers elsewhere in the Roman Catholic Church, the hierarchy in Rome had become a cesspool.

---

[13] Simony is the sale of church offices for money.

7

The High Middle Ages

AD 1000–1300

We saw a portion of the 1000 to 1300 period in the previous chapter from the perspective of the papacy and its struggle for control of the Middle East. While those events were important, they were only tangential to the restructuring of Europe and its emergence from the bleakness of the Early Middle Ages. There was a societal reorganization as well as an intellectual rebirth beginning in Europe. Part of the latter was happening in secular society, but much of it was occurring within the Catholic Church, which was growing in its domination of the continent.[1]

Feudalism

The institution that we call "feudalism" arose under the Carolingians. It was a structure of interlocking lieges. Beginning with the king, each of his underlings owed a duty to their lord to provide supplies and military support. An assortment of dukes, margraves, landgraves, counts, barons and knights linked the king to the peasants. The incumbent (i.e., liege) at each level in the hierarchy owed the land he ruled to the next highest rank. This locked every-

---

[1] Engelbrecht, *Church History*, 90–157.
Schaff, *History of the Christian Church*, vol. 4, 5.
Aland, *A History of Christianity*, Vol. 1, 215–413.
Daileader, *The High Middle Ages*.
Armstrong, *The Medieval World, Lect. 14, 16, 21, 29, 33–36.*

body into their social status, which could only be escaped by favorable marriages or warfare. Obviously, there was a great incentive to engage in both. The men in this feudal web structure were referred to as "those who fought." It was their duty to protect those under them from their adversaries.

At the bottom of this structure were the people referred to as "those who worked." The peasants and craftsmen were not really owned by their lord as if they were slaves, but they were bound to the land of their lord. Some worked the land, and some performed crafts, but all their efforts accrued to the benefit of their lord. They could not sell their wares to others. The lords owned the villages in which the people lived, although some towns, where it was to the advantage of everyone, were "free" cities. In these, merchants and tradesmen could practice their crafts without undo interference from the neighboring lords. Trade benefited the lords financially, but it decreased their direct power, so there was a tenuous equilibrium in which these towns existed.

The third class of people were "those who prayed." These were the various church officiants, priests, deacons, monks, friars, nuns, abbots, and bishops. Like their non-clerical counterparts, they had a sworn loyalty to those above them in their ecclesial group. Some of them performed the office of the ministry, but others worked with their hands or begged to support themselves. One of the two troubling issues with those who prayed was the general lack of education of many priests and even monks, a problem which had existed since the fourth century. The other continuing headache was whether clergy could marry. Although church council after church council had opposed such marriages, the issue always reappeared within a generation or two and sometimes marriages of the clergy were widely accepted.

Changes in the Norse

During the ninth and ten centuries, the Viking sea-kings had been the bane of Christian Europe.[2] They raided France, Germany, and the British Isles continually and elsewhere occasionally. They pillaged, stole, destroyed, and killed. There was no question that they were brave and skilled at navigating the North Sea, the Baltic Sea, and the Atlantic Ocean. They discovered and settled Iceland. In fact, Iceland became a center for recording Norse history and literature. They discovered and temporarily settled Greenland. They even

---

[2] Harl, *The Vikings*, Lect. 23–35.

reached the shores of North America, but they were too far away from their home bases to remain for long.

By the beginning of the eleventh century, the conditions among the Vikings were changing. In the British Isles and northern France, Viking clans were becoming settlers and taking land from the locals. They began to convert to Christianity, which put a stop to their raiding and pillaging. In the East, however, things were still more fluid. The Vikings used their boats (see chapter 5) that could travel rivers as well as seas to penetrate western Russia. In fact, the name "Russia" comes from the Vikings who were known in eastern Europe as the "Russ." Vikings penetrated southward all the way to Constantinople and became major traders along the rivers of western Russia. They captured and sold Poles as slaves to the Muslims in what is now Turkey in exchange for money and manufactured goods which they transported back to Scandinavia. As more Vikings settled among the Slavic people, the Russ wanted to find a religion to help them unite themselves with the local population. They chose Byzantine Christianity instead of Roman Christianity or Islam, which explains why Russia and Ukraine are Orthodox Christian today.

The Norman Conquest of England

For centuries the political situation in the British Isles had been a complex struggle for control between the Anglo-Saxons centered in Wessex, various Viking groups, and the Celts of Scotland and Wales. Meanwhile, on the northern coast of France, the Vikings had become the rulers and were known as the "Normans." Nominally under the French king, they were effectively an entity unto themselves. The rulers of the English, the Norwegians, the Danes, and the Normans at times intermarried to establish political alliances. This gave members of the various ruling families claims against landed positions,[3] including that of king, in the other countries.

In 1016 the Danes conquered England and made it part of their kingdom, which nominally also embraced Norway. The Danes were wracked with internal problems, however, and were thus forced to govern England through subservient kings. Eventually, the Danes lost their grip on England, and Edward

---

[3] A "landed position" was a fief that a family held which was passed on to the nearest heir when the owner died. The most usual heir was the oldest son, but if there were no sons, other males in the family tree or daughters might inherit, often leading to messy claims and counterclaims to the land and to the associated title.

the Confessor came to the throne in 1042. When he died in January 1066, there were three claimants to the English throne. They were Harold Godwinson, Harold III of Norway, and William the Bastard of Normandy. Harold Godwinson, being in England, was granted the throne by the Witan,[4] and the other claimants prepared to attack England to enforce their claims. Faced with two invasions, King Harold raced north to defeat and kill his Norwegian rival as he landed on English soil at the end of September. While Harold was in the north, William landed in Sussex and prepared to meet Harold in battle. Harold and his army returned southward after his victory over the Vikings. The battle between the two forces lasted most of the day, but the tired and outnumbered English army gave way, and Harold was killed.

The Norman conquest of England had consequences for centuries. Norman nobles moved to take over as much English land as they could, but they were resented at various levels by the English people. Moreover, because they tried to retain their holdings in northern France as well, they were often absentee landowners. William obtained the new nickname of "the Conqueror." He was king of England, but he was still a vassal to the king of France in Normandy. The issue of split loyalties would trouble English-French relations for many years. It also created a marked division between the French-speaking lords and English-speaking peasants.

France

At the beginning of the eleventh century, France was highly divided among and within warring families. Although France had kings, they were dependent on marriage alliances and military force to maintain control of even a fraction of the country. After William's conquest of England, the English kings ruled large sections of western France, supposedly as vassals, but often as more powerful neighbors of the kings of France.

Wars of this period were primarily struggles between cadres of mounted knights rather than battles between national armies. The knights were accompanied by small groups of foot soldiers who were bound to their lords by feudal oaths These private armies lived off the land, so there was frequent plundering of the peasants and the townspeople. One reason for the crusades was

---

[4] The Witan, or Witenagemot, was the royal advisory council to the Anglo-Saxon kings. It was usually attended by the greater nobles and bishops.

the pope's desire to reduce this Christian-on-Christian warfare that made Europe so unstable.

The situation in France changed with the coronation of Philip II, who reigned from 1179 to 1223. King Philip conspired with Richard Lionheart, the son of King Henry II of England, to defeat Richard's father in France. Philip gained some territory from Richard, who having defeated his father, became king of England. The alliance between Philip and Richard broke down during the Third Crusade, however, and Richard captured almost all of France. Richard soon thereafter was killed fighting his own vassals, and Philip recaptured much of France from the English King John, who succeeded Richard, as we see in the next paragraph. Philip's successors were able to keep together the portion of France that they held and to expand their holdings to the south through marriage and timely deaths. France looked like a piece of Swiss cheese with a growing portion in the hands of the French king, but significant portions in the hands of others.

The Magna Carta

King Henry II of England, father of Richard Lionheart, had been successful in his warfare in France, but he faced rebellion by three of his five sons. Two were killed but, as noted above, Richard took the throne of England from his father. Another brother of Richard was Prince John, who became regent of England while his brother went on the Third Crusade. This was the era when Robin Hood supposedly lived in England, battling the forces of the "wicked Prince John" in the name of King Richard. After John became king, he lost much of his land in France to Philip II (see previous section), and he also incurred large debts in the process.

Many of the English nobles had also lost land in France and were angry with King John, whom they blamed for the losses and for the high taxes. They fomented a revolt, and John's situation was not good. After the rebels captured London, John was forced to ask Stephen Langton, the Archbishop of Canterbury, to help mediate a settlement. At Runnymede on June 10, 1215, John and the nobles signed the Magna Carta, giving the nobles essential rights vis-à-vis the king. John, of course, had no intention of keeping the provisions of the document, and he asked the pope to annul it. After only three months, the battle between the nobles and King John resumed, and the rebels sought help from the king of France. John soon died, leaving his nine-year-old son,

Henry III, on the throne. Although civil strife continued periodically during the following years, the Magna Carta became a more and more important part of English life before Henry III was old enough to rule on his own. While the struggle between king and nobles continued in various forms over many years, the general principles stated in the Magna Carta remained in force and became part of English common law.

Hispania

After Muslim forces captured Hispania but were blunted in their attempt to capture France, the tide of the struggle for Hispania gradually turned in favor of the Christians. Christian rulers in southern France were able to expel the Muslims that had moved north out of the Pyrenees. Progressively, Christians gained control of the Pyrenees as the Muslims in Hispania became involved in internal disputes, some of which reached all the way back to their nominal capital of Bagdad. By the beginning of the High Middle ages in 1000, several Christian kingdoms existed in the northeastern portion of the peninsula. Over the next three hundred years, much of the center of Spain, as well as most of what is now Portugal, came under Christian rule. Wars involved local states, sometimes with the backing of Christian rulers in Europe and of Muslim rulers in North Africa and the Middle East. For both sides, however, Hispania was a backwater, not a central theater of action.

Empire Versus Papacy

To paraphrase the eighteenth century French philosopher Voltaire and others, the Holy Roman Empire (HRE) was not holy, not really an empire, and only sometimes included Rome. It generally ran from Denmark to Rome and from eastern France to the Czech Republic. Like all the other nations of Europe, it was often divided into warring factions. The HRE had a special relationship with the popes in Rome, however, and it was not always pleasant. In particular, HRE rulers had significant authority until the eleventh century to appoint bishops and abbots in their territories because these officials often had temporal as well as religious power. The monarchs gave these church leaders the symbols of their offices, such as the vestments, staffs, and miters. An even greater issue was whether the Holy Roman Emperor selected, or at least approved of the selection of the pope, or whether the pope selected and crowned the emperor, or at least approved of his selection before his coronation. The struggle became known as the Investiture Controversy, and it broke into open conflict in 1076 between Pope Gregory VII, whom we met in the last chapter, and Emperor Henry IV.

Hildebrand, before becoming Gregory VII, ignited the controversy in 1059 by guiding the papal decisions to declare that the emperor had no role in selecting the pope and to reconstitute the College of Cardinals. As pope himself in 1075, he declared that only the pope could appoint and depose emperors. In the short term, the pope had the advantage because Henry was tied up with civil wars. In 1081 Henry attacked Rome, and the Vatican fell under his control in 1083. Gregory was forced to flee, but he was brought back to Rome by the Normans. He soon was driven out again and died (see chapter 6). Eventually, Henry V and Pope Callixtus II signed the Concord of Worms to settle the matter. A similar struggle occurred between the papacy and England and was also settled by a concord. This latter concord had only a limited impact, owing to the distance between Rome and London. The Concord of Worms, however, weakened the emperor, delaying the unification of Germany and Italy until the nineteenth century. The struggle between the popes and the emperors did not go away, but the pope's hand was definitely strengthened in future disagreements due to the actions of Gregory VII and Callixtus II.[5]

Heresies

The **Waldensians** were a group that originated at Lyon, France, in 1173. They were founded by Peter Waldo, a prosperous merchant who gave away his wealth to live in apostolic poverty. His followers were first called the "poor men of Lyon." The group was declared heretical in 1215 and was intensively and brutally persecuted. Because the church was extremely jealous of its power, it did not want laymen establishing their own doctrine and practice. The Waldensians wanted the Bible in the language and in the hands of the common people, which at the time was regarded as sacrilege by the church. Despite being persecuted, the movement spread across southern France and into Italy. Its teachings developed over time and eventually became similar to those of other Protestant groups. Many Waldensians eventually became Calvinists.

---

[5]   Readers may want to reread the relevant parts of chapters 6 and 7 because the relationship between the popes and the emperors needs to be considered from both sides.

A far greater threat to the church was posed by the **Cathars**. Exactly where they came from is unclear. It is likely their founders were the remnants of some Gnostic sect that had never been completely eradicated in the hinterland of the Balkans. Eventually, they found their way to southeastern France and northwestern Italy (always a hotbed for dissidents) and tried to spread up the Rhine and even into England. By the middle of the twelfth century, they became numerous enough to attract the attention of the church. Cathars were dualists, believing in two gods, one good and the other evil. They believed in Jesus Christ but not in his incarnation. They grew in strength during the twelfth century, and in 1208 Pope Innocent III launched the Albigensian Crusade to suppress them. In contrast to the Waldensians, the church regarded Cathars not as heretics but as pagans to be killed or driven out of Europe. Also, unlike the humble Waldensians, the Cathars were prepared to fight for their survival and to make alliances with the lords of the land to do so. The response of the church was brutal, killing them wherever they could be found. They were finally wiped out in 1321.

Scholasticism

During the Early Middle Ages, intellectual activity within the general population and within the church greatly declined. Many of the books of the Roman era had been destroyed in the West, and those which remained were frequently hidden in monasteries for safety. There they lay forgotten, rotting, and being destroyed by rodents and other vermin. In the eleventh century, things began to turn around as cathedral schools[6] were established in Italy, France, and England. This led to the birth of scholastic theology, which was an attempt to reconcile reason and faith. In particular, scholasticism tried to explain biblical theology through Aristotelian logic and the writings of the early Church Fathers. An underlying principle was that all forms of truth were interrelated, and therefore each truth could be found through the study of others. Scholasticism led to each verse of Scripture being given four meanings and to an overemphasizing of form instead of substance. Let us consider a few of the great theologians of this era.

Anselm of Canterbury (1033–1109) was born in northwestern Italy. Due to the political struggles at the time, his early life was not easy or tranquil. He

---

[6]   Cathedral schools were centers of advanced learning to serve the church and state.

wandered around France for five years before becoming a Benedictine monk in the monastery at Bec.[7] In 1063 he was elected prior of the monastery and later became its abbot. After a long political delay caused by King William II of England, Anselm was installed as Archbishop of Canterbury in 1093. As archbishop he resolutely maintained the church's right to choose its bishops and place men into other church positions. For this resistance to royal encroachment into the business of the church, he was exiled from England twice, once by William II and once by Henry I.

Anselm has been called "the Father of Scholasticism." His works are considered philosophical as well as theological because he tried to rationalize the teachings of the Christian church, which had traditionally been considered to be revealed truth. His view of the intellectual world followed the Neoplatonism of St. Augustine, but Anselm also became interested in the logic and thought of Aristotle. He thereby opened the door for French philosophers of the next century to introduce all the trappings of Aristotle's system of thought into the church. Anselm's course of study led him to argue that once faith is held fast, one must attempt to demonstrate its truth by means of reason. Driven by this idea, he argued that man could prove the existence of God through logic. His argument was fallacious, as have been all the arguments for the existence of God proposed since his time.

Peter Lombard (1096–1160) was born in poverty in northwestern Italy and educated in the neighboring cathedral schools.[8] After gaining the patronage of a local bishop, he was able to move to the cathedral school in Reims and later to the one in Paris. By 1145 he was a professor at the cathedral school of Notre Dame. He subsequently moved up the Paris church ranks, becoming a sub-deacon, deacon, and then archdeacon by 1152. He was elected bishop in 1159, but he died a year later.

Peter Lombard is most famous for his *Four Books of Sentences* which earned him the title "Master of the Sentences." These books of biblical commentary became the framework for the next four centuries of scholastic interpretation of the Bible and were even used by Luther in his university studies. They were a compilation of biblical texts, with relevant passages from the church fathers and medieval thinkers. The Trinity was covered in Book I, cre-

---

[7]   John Fortin, ed., *Saint Anselm: His Origins and Influence* (Lewiston, New York: Edwin Mellen Press, 2001).
[8]   Marcia L. Colish, *Peter Lombard*, Vols. 1, 2 (New York: E. J. Brill, 1994).

ation in Book II, the person and office of Christ in Book III, and the sacraments in Book IV. Lombard also wrote commentaries on the Pauline epistles and the Psalms. His writings were not without controversy. In Book I, Lombard identified charity with the Holy Spirit. He claimed that when the Christian loves God and his neighbor, this love literally is God. In other words, the Christian becomes divine and is taken up into the life of the Trinity. The Catholic Church never accepted that concept, but it did eventually accede to his teaching on marriage. He taught that marriage was consensual and need not be consummated to be considered perfect and absolutely indissoluble.

Thomas Aquinas, (1225–1274) was born in southern Italy into a powerful family.[9] He studied at several places, but especially at Naples, and from there was recruited to join the Dominican monastic order. After escaping his family's efforts to prevent him from becoming a Dominican, he arrived safely in Rome and was then sent to Paris in 1245. Following years of study in Paris and Cologne, he became a doctor of theology and taught in Paris. In 1259 he returned to Italy, held various teaching posts and became the papal theologian. The Dominicans sent him to Paris in 1269 for several years, but he returned to Italy in 1272 and died two years later as the result of an accident on his way to the Second Council of Lyon.

Thomas Aquinas was an outspoken proponent of natural theology and the father of Thomism, a philosophy that argues that reason is found in God. Aquinas strongly embraced key ideas of Aristotle and attempted to unite Aristotelian philosophy with the principles of Christianity. Martin Luther would vehemently oppose this idea. Aquinas's best-known works are *Disputed Questions on Truth*, the *Summa Contra Gentiles,* and his massively influential *Summa Theologica*. He wrote numerous commentaries on the Scriptures and on Aristotle. Thomas Aquinas is considered one of the Catholic Church's greatest theologians and philosophers.

John Duns Scotus (1266–1308) was a Scottish priest and Franciscan friar.[10] Nothing is known about his life before his ordination as a priest in 1291. At some point he became a Franciscan monk, and he began to work at Oxford in

---

[9] Nicholas M. Healy, *Thomas Aquinas: Theologian of the Christian Life* (Farnham, UK: Ashgate Publishing, 2003).

[10] Allan B. Wolter, *The Philosophical Theology of John Duns Scotus* (Ithaca: Cornell University Press, 1990).

1300. He made several trips to France and lectured on Peter Lombard's *Sentences* in 1304. He died unexpectedly in Cologne in 1308.

Scotus's great work is his commentary on the *Sentences*. He wrote on both religion and philosophy and, as was common at his time, often improperly mixed them. Much of his writing is difficult for non-philosophers to grasp.[11] Scotus also developed a complicated argument for the existence of God that, of course, was logically flawed. He supported the early pseudo-Christian literature argument for the immaculate conception of Mary. He is sometimes referred to as the "Subtle Doctor" of the Roman church.

First Universities

In 1079 Pope Gregory VII issued a decree concerning the establishment of cathedral schools for the training of men for service in the church. From some of these schools the first universities in Europe arose—in Barcelona (1088), in Paris (1150) and in Oxford (1167). While the curricula were heavily influenced by the needs of the church, secular subjects were soon also being taught. The translation of Aristotle into Latin and the growing scholastic theological movement added material to the curriculum. Universities received funds from the local rulers and were sanctioned by the church, but they quickly tried to loosen their bonds to these estates. Recruiting paying students was a way to gain independence, so students from wealthy families were sought. What was taught was often dependent on who was available to teach. If professors moved from one school to another, many of their students often went with them.

The Resurgence of Monasticism

Monasticism had begun in the Western church in the fourth century, and the Rule of St. Benedict had become the dominant standard of behavior as monasteries were formed in France and Ireland. At the start of the eleventh century, new monastic orders began to appear. This wave was boosted by the crusader orders in which monks were also knights. During this period the Rule of St. Augustine became more popular and was adopted by numerous orders. Monastic orders could be formed only with the approval of the pope.

---

[11] Perhaps this is why "Duns" led to the word "dunce."

A new and controversial order called the Franciscan order was founded by **Francis of Assisi** (1181–1226) in 1209. For several years before this date, he had been preaching in the vicinity of Rome, trying to impress upon Pope Innocent III that people should live in the manner of Jesus, owning nothing and begging or working for food.[12] To Francis this lifestyle was the way to true holiness before God. The pope was not impressed, but finally relented and let Francis create his new order. Discipline was strict, and monks often appeared half-starved. They were referred to as the "barefoot friars" (preachers) in some places because they were too poor to even own a pair of sandals.

A host of new orders appeared in the twelfth and thirteenth century as more and more people sought to enter monasteries and convents because the church promoted monasticism as the only sure way of salvation. Since the monastic orders were directly answerable to the pope, more monks increased the pressure that the pope could bring to bear on secular rulers who disagreed with him.

The High Middle Ages were a relatively good period for Europe. The population grew steadily, learning returned, and states became better organized. The church also became stronger. Alas, for Europe and for the church, all of this was about to change with the start of the fourteenth century.

---

[12]   John R. H. Moorman, *Saint Francis of Assisi* (St. Bonaventure, New York: Franciscan Institute Publications, 1987).

8

The Late Middle Ages
AD 1300–1500

The fourteenth century started with a struggle between a French king and a pope, and it went downhill quickly from there, both in the church and in society.[1]

The "Babylonian Captivity"[2]

The popes had gradually been getting the upper hand against the German emperors in the previous period, but Pope Boniface VIII met his match in King Philip IV of France. Boniface was elected after his predecessor had resigned, and Philip questioned Boniface's legitimacy. A war of words became legal charges and worse, until the king kidnapped the pope. Although Boniface soon was freed, he died the next month. He was succeeded by Benedict XI, who died within a year.

The next pope was Clement V. He had been the archbishop of Bordeaux, and he chose never to go to Rome. Instead, he set up his papal court at Avignon in southern France in 1309. The popes remained in France until 1377.

---

[1] Engelbrecht, *Church History*, 158–205.

   Schaff, *History of the Christian Church*, Vol. 6.

   Aland, *A History of Christianity*, Vol. 1, 337–413.

   Philip Daileader, *The Late Middle Ages* (Chantilly, Virginia: The Great Courses Teaching Company, 2007).

[2] This term has been applied to the period during which the popes resided in Avignon, which was about the same length of time that the Jews were held captive in Babylon.

Clement had several reasons for staying away from Rome. Rome was uncomfortable in the summer, and the Roman political environment was often toxic for popes due to the struggles among Italian noble families for control of the papacy. The critical events in Europe were happening in France, and Clement thought it best that he remained close to them. Because he appointed numerous French cardinals, it was natural that they would elect popes who also liked the south of France.

The first big issue Clement faced was the desire of Philip IV to dissolve the Knights Templar, an organization of French knights which was formed during the crusades. The knights had become rich through banking, and Philip, deeply in debt to them, wanted the money. He pressured the pope to permit him to seize and execute all the leaders of the order. Clement's successors remained in France because there were political struggles within France in which they had an interest. Thereafter, the outbreak of the Hundred Years War between France and England gave the pope an incentive to remain nearby to pressure the combatants to reduce the senseless violence.

Dissenting Theologians

While the popes enjoyed the south of France, two English theologians arose who would disturb the era of scholasticism.

William of Ockham[3] was a Franciscan monk from Ockham in Surrey. Born in 1285, this scholastic theologian would die in Munich in 1347. He attended Oxford and eventually became an instructor there. He wrote commentaries on Peter Lombard's *Sentences*, but some of these were controversial. As a result, he was sent to the papal court at Avignon for trial in 1327. Matters took a weird turn when the pope attacked the Rule of St. Francis. Ockham, as he is always referred to, fled to the court of Holy Roman Emperor Louis IV of Bavaria. He was excommunicated but lived under the protection of Louis with other renegade Franciscans. He wrote arguments supporting Louis IV's position against the pope, who was safely in France and not in Louis's territory.

Ockham argued that the ways of God are not discernable by reason; they had to be revealed to men through the Scriptures. In this he foreshadowed Martin Luther, who also argued that the God of our salvation could not be

---

[3] Paul Spade, *The Cambridge Companion to Ockham* (Cambridge: Cambridge University Press, 1999).

known except from the Bible. On the other hand, Ockham was a Semi-Pelagian in his view of how man is saved, putting the emphasis on man acting first to gain God's grace. This was in stark contrast to Thomas Aquinas, who argued that God had to act first. Among Ockham's philosophical writings, he is best known for a principle called "Ockham's Razor." It states that if there are several possible answers to a question or several explanations for a natural phenomenon, the correct answer or explanation is the one which requires the fewest assumptions. Ockham's Razor is not a law of nature, and it is only sometimes true, but many people strongly believe in it.

John Wycliffe (1328–1384) was born in Yorkshire,[4] but little is known about his early life. He got a bachelor's degree from Oxford in 1356, after living through the years of the Black Death (see below). He worked as a teacher, a writer, and a priest in the vicinity of Oxford. He continued his studies until he received his doctorate in 1372. He soon became embroiled in church politics, as he wrote treatises against some of the abuses in the church. He also led an effort to translate the Vulgate into Middle English, producing the Wycliffe Bible. All this activity got him into deeper trouble with the church which wanted to retain control over doctrine and not to have the Bible in the hands of the laity. Although condemned by the pope and several councils, he managed to survive until he died of natural causes in 1384.

Wycliffe attacked both the abuses in the church and its doctrine. In the latter, he foreshadowed Martin Luther to a large extent. He claimed that the Bible was the only source of doctrine. He attacked the sacramental system and transubstantiation. He advocated predestination and the concept of the invisible church. He rejected purgatory, pilgrimages to shrines, indulgences, and prayers to the saints. He encouraged the selling of excess church property and the deposing of the church hierarchy. He also taught the concept of "dominion," i.e., that only those who are in a state of grace have the right to exercise authority and hold property. This teaching had troubling implications for the political sphere. It is likely that only the turmoil caused by the war between England and France and the existence of two contending popes, one in Rome and one at Avignon, prevented him from being executed. While we see similarities between Wycliffe and Luther, the former was likely closer to John Calvin in his views on theology and the church.

---

[4]   Gordon Leff, *John Wyclif: The Path of Dissent* (Oxford: Oxford University Press, 1966).

The Black Death

At the beginning of the fourteenth century, Europe was unable to reliably feed its population. Good weather and better farming methods in the previous century had led more land to be brought under cultivation. This, however, caused a problem. Some of the new land was marginal, and when years of bad weather struck in the first third of the fourteenth century, there were famines. These conditions weakened many and caused others to die. The Great Famine of 1315 killed at least 5% of the European population.

Suddenly, there appeared what at the time was called the "Great Mortality," but what is today referred to as the "Black Death." It began in modern-day Kyrgyzstan in central Asia in 1338 and worked its way west over the next decade. It may have spread east and south as well. It reached the Mediterranean Basin in 1347 and spread northward during the next four years. It caused at least 30% of the European population to die. The mortality was much greater in the south of Europe than the north because this plague flourished in warmer areas. The whole population of some cities died, and large areas were depopulated. Many thought that it was the hand of God punishing mankind for its sins. When the plague finally abated, it was not gone permanently. Periodically, it would return in weaker but still deadly form.

The plague was caused by the bacterium *Yersinia pestis*, and it appeared in three forms. In its most common form, it developed black tumors, or buboes, on the limbs of the body. Thus, it has been called the "bubonic plague." This form was caused by being bitten by fleas which were common on ground rodents, particularly rats. The other two forms of the plague killed even more quickly. It was possible to inhale the bacteria directly into the lungs, referred to as "pneumatic." It killed people within a couple of days. It was also possible to get the bacteria directly into the bloodstream through breaks in the skin. This was called "septicemic" and was fatal within a day. People did not know the cause of the disease and tried all sorts of remedies, such as carrying flowers to sniff to avoid the bad air and "bleeding" to get the evil fluids out of the body.

After the Great Mortality, underproductive land was abandoned, and wages rose because the reduction in workers increased the demand for their labor. The conditions of the lower classes improved as a result. On the other hand, respect for the state and the church weakened because neither was able to do anything to stop the plague.

The Hundred Years War (1337–1453)

The recurring wars between England and France that began after William conquered England in 1066 reached their most deadly period during the Hundred Years War. Ever since William the Conqueror seized the English throne, the English king had owned land in France as well as in England. These holdings had been greatly reduced by losses that had occurred under King John of England at the beginning of the thirteenth century, but they did not completely disappear. The kings of France, however, were interested in pushing the English out, which is exactly what King Philip VI tried to do to King Edward III of England. The English struck back, and the fighting continued, with numerous truces, for 116 years before the French finally were able to defeat the English. It is important to realize how much history happened during this war. It started during the Babylonian Captivity of the papacy. The Black Death came and went. The Papal Schism occurred, and the Council of Constance was held. The Renaissance began in Italy.

The most remembered episode of the war was the rise and subsequent death of **Joan of Arc** (1412–1431).[5] She was born into a relatively poor family in the northeast of France. By the time she was a teenager, she claimed that she was seeing visions. Eventually, these visions directed her to go to the yet-uncrowned King Charles VII of France. He was not impressed by her. Nevertheless, because his own efforts to prevent being driven from France by King Henry VI of England were unsuccessful, Charles sent her with a relief army to lift the siege of Orleans. Dressed in armor, she inspired the French defenders and quickly freed the city. A year later, however, she was captured by the army of Burgundy and turned over to the English. She was condemned as a heretic by a bishop loyal to the English and burned at the stake. Years later, she was acclaimed a hero of the French and made a saint.

The Papal Schism

The people of Rome were hurt financially by the departure of the pope to France. They began a lobbying campaign throughout Europe to force the Bishop of Rome to return to Rome. Pope Gregory XI and his court did return to Rome in 1377 for a visit, and he had the misfortune of dying there. The people of Rome were quick to seize the opportunity to put one of their own

---

[5]   Edward Lucie-Smith, *Joan of Arc* (Bristol: Allen Lane, 1976).

on the papal throne. Under threats from the people of Rome, the cardinals elected an Italian who took the name Urban VI. He, however, was so ill-tempered and reformist that the cardinals regretted their decision. They left Rome and elected a man from Geneva who took the name Clement VII and moved to Avignon. There were now two popes, both elected by some of the same cardinals. The papal split caused people in the various countries to choose between the rivals. This led to mass disruption within the parishes and monasteries, as people disputed who the real pope was. Each pope died and was replaced. After the new popes refused to meet, the cardinals from each side met in Pisa. They voted to depose both of them and elect a different man to be pope. They elected Alexander V, who quickly died and was succeeded by John XXIII.[6] As a result, there were three popes.

It was clear that the only way to resolve this dispute was open warfare or a church council. A movement called "conciliarism" began to arise among both the laity and some of the clergy. Despite this, since neither the pope at Rome nor the one at Avignon were willing to call a council, the effort was stalemated. Finally, John XXIII agreed to call a council, which met at Constance in Switzerland in 1414. The actions of the council, meeting on the soil of the Holy Roman Empire, would be momentous.

Church Corruption

During the Late Middle Ages, corruption in the Roman church reached unimaginable heights. Some of the evils were presented in the stories in Giovanni Boccaccio's *The Decameron*.[7] Many involved the dubious religious and sexual practices of the clergy. It was claimed by some that everyone from the pope to the parish priest had a wench, and the honorable clerics had only one. Celibacy was formally required, but seldom practiced. The offices of bishops and above were often regarded as private possessions by the rich families into which they might place a second-born or third-born son for the purpose of ruling both civil and ecclesiastical territories and profiting from them. Many of these men were not suited to church life and continued to live the life of their

---

[6] This pope named John XXIII is, of course, not the same man who was pope under that name in the twentieth century. Because the first pope by that name was regarded as an "antipope" by the Catholic Church, the name was available to be used again by a legitimate pope.

[7] Giovanni Boccaccio, *The Decameron*, trans. G. H. McWilliam (Franklin Center, Pennsylvania: The Franklin Library, 1981).

wealthy relatives, numerous of whom had several female partners. To keep the ranks of the lower clergy full, the practice of licensing concubines for priests continued under the argument that it was a better solution than allowing priests to commit fornication and adultery among their parishioners. It did not always work.

Simony, the sale of clerical positions to the highest bidder, and the bending of church laws for money were also common. The higher clergy needed money for their lifestyles and for building massive churches and monasteries. That money had to come from somewhere. This situation was used to entice powerful secular families to buy high church offices which permitted them to extend their power into the religious lives of their subjects. Bishoprics were being filled by rich men who had little interest in things spiritual, but who desired the income from the lands belonging to the church.

There were no "collection plates" in Medieval churches to obtain funds from the attendees.[8] To extract money from the poor as well as the rich, the Catholic Church made extensive use of the sacramental system and the sale of indulgences. This led to the wholesale manufacturing of phony relics and false documents. The relics were used in the "pay-for-view" business run by many churches and cathedrals, where the parishioners could gain an indulgence by viewing a relic and making a contribution for the privilege. The church used the forgery of documents to back up its various claims of authority over the state and the affairs of its members. Some monasteries specialized in producing false relics and phony documents, often claiming that they had special connections in the eastern empire through which they were able to obtain these "rare treasures."

However, the practices of the Roman Church did not go unchallenged during this period. William of Ockham and John Wycliffe had raised questions about the church's doctrine and practices. It was, however, **Jan Hus**,[9] the "Bohemian Goose,"[10] who caused the greatest concern to the papists. Hus (1372–1415) was born to poor Bohemian parents and studied for the priesthood to gain a way to make a living. He went to Prague, where he completed his training and was ordained after earning a bachelor-of-arts degree. He preached in Prague, and his preaching was anything but orthodox. He was ex-

---

[8] Collection plates were an American invention out of necessity since the church had no other sources of funds.

[9] Count Lützow, *Life & Times of Master John Hus* (London: E. P. Dutton & Co., 1909).

[10] "Hus" referred to himself as a "goose," from the meaning of his name.

communicated by Alexander V and by John XXIII and forced to go into exile. Hus's issues involved both the lack of doctrinal integrity and the corruption in the church. He circulated the banned writings of John Wycliffe, and his theological positions were generally consistent with those of Wycliffe. Hus was invited under a safe-conduct document signed by the emperor to present his views at the Council of Constance.

Council of Constance

The council, which had been pushed by the conciliar movement, convened in Constance, Germany, in 1414 and continued until 1418.[11] Relatively few bishops attended, but many doctors of theology and doctors of the Canon Law came, as did representatives of universities, cathedral schools and secular rulers. King Sigismund, ruler of Hungary and future Holy Roman Emperor, attended and was influential. The primary purpose of the council was to end the Great Schism by deposing all three current popes and naming a new one. Nothing was simple. There were arguments over how the voting would be done, and it was decided that each "nation" would have one vote. When the council asked all three popes to resign, John XXIII, the only pope in attendance, fled and removed the authority of the council. Pope Gregory XII of Rome sent a letter reauthorizing the council and then resigned. John XXIII was forced to resign and fled into exile in Austria. Benedict XIII refused to resign and took secluded refuge in Spain. The council delayed electing Martin V as pope until near the end of its sessions to prevent the new pope from interfering with the council.

The council then heard the charges against Jan Hus, who had been summoned to the council under the previously mentioned pledge of safe conduct from the emperor. After the council condemned the teachings of John Wycliffe, it also condemned the teachings of Hus and of Jerome of Prague. The latter two men, despite their safe conduct documents, were then handed over to the civil authorities and were both burned at the stake.

The council required, as a condition of his appointment, that Pope Martin V accept the need to call regular councils whose decisions were to be the supreme authority within the church. The next several popes worked quickly to escape that encumbrance and reassert their rule over the whole church.

---

[11] Philip Stump, *The Reforms of the Council of Constance (1414–1418)* (Boston: Brill Publishers, 1994).

The Hussite Wars

The death of Jan Hus caused outrage among the people of Bohemia. Hus had trained numerous preachers, and they continued to teach his doctrines after his death. King Wenceslaus IV of Bohemia hoped to become Holy Roman Emperor and therefore tried to stamp out the rebellion. When he died a few years later, his brother Sigismund continued the effort to forcibly end the Hussite rebellion. Between 1419 and 1434 the popes authorized three crusades to be launched against the Hussites, with knights coming from all over Europe to participate. Each crusade failed, and the Hussites responded by plundering areas of nearby Saxony. The memory of this would turn Duke George of Saxony against Martin Luther when the latter affirmed some of Hus's teachings.

The fighting ended when the Catholic rulers concluded they had better things to do and after the Hussites were exhausted from the constant warfare. A treaty allowed the Hussites to keep most of their religious practices in exchange for their accepting the overlordship of the emperor and the pope.

Christians Versus Muslims

The Muslims had taken northern Africa, Hispania, and Sicily before the High Middle Ages and had been pressuring the Byzantine Empire for centuries.[12] Sicily, however, had been cleared of Muslims in the eleventh century by the Normans. In the East, the Byzantines had been gradually worn down by the Ottoman Turks. By 1453 almost the only thing that remained for them was their capital at Constantinople. The city seemed impregnable, but the Turks used two new ploys to capture it. First, they slid some of their ships over the isthmus behind Constantinople so they could attack it from its undefended coast. Secondly, they obtained a huge cannon from a Hungarian cannon-maker. This cannon was able to break down the thick walls of the city. It is ironic that the Byzantines could have bought the cannon before it was offered to the Muslims, but they thought it was too expensive.

In Hispania, it was the Christians who were on the offensive. By the beginning of the fourteenth century, Portugal and all of Spain, except for Granada, were under Christian control. Over this period the Christian kingdoms gradually reorganized themselves through marriage and warfare into the precursors of the modern state of Spain. The size of Granada was gradually reduced by

---

[12] Gearon, *Turning Points*, Lect. 19–23.

Christian pressure. In 1469 Ferdinand of Aragon married Isabella of Castile. When each of them became monarch of their respective kingdoms, the nation of Spain was effectively formed. These rulers soon launched the Spanish Inquisition to stamp out all religious dissent. It was used to identify Christian heretics, Jews whose conversion was suspect, and any other religious opponents of their version of Catholicism. On January 2, 1492, the last Muslim ruler of Granada surrendered, and Spain was reunited under Christian rule. A few months thereafter, Ferdinand and Isabella sent Christopher Columbus to seek a new sea route to the Orient.

Italian Renaissance

The Black Death in the fourteenth century had decimated Italy. Amazingly, relative prosperity returned quickly to the city-states that occupied northern Italy. Particularly in the city of Florence, where money was to be made in commercial trading, men began trying their hand at painting and writing.[13] Giotto di Bondone introduced realism into painting through his use of shading. Francesco Petrarch rediscovered many lost works of the Roman authors and wrote works of his own in the flowing Latin of the ancients. The chancellor of Florence and the de Medici family became patrons of the arts. Giovanni Boccaccio wrote the major literary work entitled *The Decameron*, which described life at the time in a hundred stories told by people who had gone into seclusion to avoid the Black Death. This book may have inspired Geoffrey Chaucer to write *The Canterbury Tales* several decades later.

The Italian writers and artists began thinking of history in three eras. The first era was occupied with the greatness of Greece and Rome. That era was followed by the decline of civilization into the Middle Ages. Finally, mankind was entering the third era, the era of the "Rebirth," when once again man would build a glorious civilization. The Renaissance marked the rebirth of classical humanism. This thinking would dominate northern Italy in the fifteenth century and spread north to France, the Low Countries, and England during the following century. Yet, with the coming of the sixteenth century, something was on the doorstep that would make the Renaissance seem tame by comparison.

---

[13]   Peter Burke, *The Italian Renaissance: Culture and Society in Italy* (Princeton: Princeton University Press, 1999).

9

The Lutheran Reformation
AD 1500–1546

It would be easy to write many chapters on the Protestant Reformation or devote this whole chapter to Luther. Then again, understanding how the Reformation played into the politics of Europe and affected the Renaissance is important for understanding why Lutheranism followed the course it did after this period. Luther's actions changed the church, but it also altered the world.[1]

Religion and Politics in the Holy Roman Empire

The fifteenth century had been one of growing corruption in the Roman Catholic Church, and the sixteenth century continued the trend. The cardinals were politicians and/or relatives of the popes. Most had little interest in church service. At the time of the election of Rodrigo de Borgia as Pope Alexander VI in 1492, only 4 of 27 cardinals were actual churchmen. Alexander had a concubine and children, one of whom was the infamous Lucrecia Borgia. He was involved in political schemes and wars, using his children as pawns and

---

[1] Engelbrecht, *Church History*, 158–205.

Schaff, *History of the Christian Church*, Vols. 6–8.

Aland, *A History of Christianity*, Vol. 2, 3–197.

Roland H. Bainton, *Here I Stand* (New York: Abingdon Press, 1950).

Ernest G. Schwiebert, *Luther and His Times* (Saint Louis: Concordia Publishing House, 1950).

Robert Kolb and James A. Nestingen, eds., *Sources and Contents of The Book of Concord*, Minneapolis: Fortress Press, 2001).

warriors. It would have been hard for a pope to be more non-religious. He was followed by other popes who also had a low regard for the purpose of the papal office. Rome had become a city in which sin of every sort was openly practiced, often by the clergy as well as the laity. In addition, the popes struggled for secular power with the Holy Roman emperors.

In 1513 the papacy fell into the hands of Leo X (1475–1521), a member of the de Medici family. Leo was essentially a Renaissance humanist, who had not been ordained as a priest before being elected pope. He had deeply imbibed of the Italian version of the Renaissance and was far more interested in art and philosophy than he was in theology. That was not surprising, given the way popes were chosen or what their role had become. He spent money recklessly and sold church offices to pay his bills.

Leo decided to build a lavish church dedicated to St. Peter, now known as St. Peter's Basilica. He needed money for the project, so he sold church offices to raise the funds. However, purchasers did not always have ready cash, so he accepted loans on their behalf from the papal bankers, the Fugger family of Augsburg, and granted the purchasers the right to sell indulgences to repay the loans. Indulgences granted remission of church punishments, as specified in the indulgence, for the living and the dead, without the need for repentance or penance.

Many people within the clergy and the educated class objected to the corruption in the church. The pope, however, held a strong hand against reform, because he could excommunicate anyone who challenged him, which carried civil as well as church penalties. Popes in the Middle Ages also used an "interdict" to penalize entire countries or regions. Sacraments were invalidated by such an "interdict," cutting off people's means of earning merit before God, so authorities were pressured by popular opinion to follow papal injunctions.

Humanism

Because many men involved in the Reformation were humanists, it is well to first consider the nature of humanism in the era of Luther. Classical humanists wanted to recreate the intellectual culture that had existed in ancient Greece and Rome. Naturally, such an approach placed a high value on human reason but also on the ability to appreciate the finer arts of painting, music, literature, and sculpture. It required a population that could speak and write with eloquence and manage the affairs of church and state with prudence and virtue. This necessitated the study of Latin and Greek, as well as of history, literature, grammar, rhetoric, and moral philosophy. Humanism placed its focus on what man could achieve. As a creature of God, he was perceived to be able to discern the ways of God through his intellect.

The revival of classical humanism began in Italy as stated in the previous chapter. By the sixteenth century, it had spread throughout Europe. The invention of the printing press by Gutenberg had made books much more available, thereby increasing the ability of humanist scholars to read works by authors from numerous eras and locations. This helped humanism awaken a love of learning among a wider swath of the population. Humanists collected books and enlarged university libraries. The influx of Byzantine scholars after the fall of Constantinople in 1453 aided in accelerating the movement.

Humanism caused changes in the scope and content of the curriculum of the schools and universities. It removed logic, but it added history and Greek and increased the prominence of poetry. The humanist educational program won rapid acceptance and by the mid-fifteenth century was well established in many places. Classical humanists did not see themselves in opposition to Christianity, but they desired to supplement it through their study by finding other ancient sources of God-inspired wisdom.

Luther, the Troubled Monk

Martin Luther was born in 1483 into a successful working-class family in Eisleben, Saxony, and grew up in Mansfield. He was the oldest of seven children. His father wanted him to go into law to better support the family. Luther therefore studied at Mansfield, Magdeburg, Eisenach and finally the university at Erfurt. Yet, he was troubled about his standing before God. Death could come at any age from any number of causes, so a person needed to always be ready to face the judgment of God. After being frightened during a thunderstorm, he vowed to enter a monastery. He chose the Augustinians in Erfurt because of their strict discipline. He worked to be the best monk possible, but he continued to fall short of what he thought God demanded. He became a priest and studied theology in the hope of finding the key to salvation.

In 1502 Frederick the Wise had established a university at Wittenberg. It grew slowly, so he tried to improve the faculty by getting professors from the

Augustinian cloister in Erfurt.[2] In 1511 Martin Luther was sent to assume that role. Soon Luther was pushed to obtain his doctorate and then to fill the Chair of the Bible at the university. Teaching the Bible made him study the Bible, not just in the context of Peter Lombard's *Sentences* (see chapter 7), but in terms of its actual text. While teaching Romans, he discovered the key to heaven that he had so long sought: "The just shall live by faith." (Romans 1:17) Placed on the right road by the Holy Spirit, Luther soon started pointing his students away from the interpretations of the church fathers to the plain meaning of the words of Scripture in context. He also became disturbed by the Dominican monk John Tetzel, who was selling indulgences nearby and causing the people of Luther's congregation to stop coming to confession. On October 31, 1517, Luther posted a challenge to debate ninety-five statements (i.e., theses) about indulgences on the door of the Castle Church in Wittenberg, a common place for posting university announcements. The world would never be the same again. The Latin theses were translated into German and spread across northern Europe. Soon Luther was challenging other Catholic teachings, and the church began to take notice.

Luther's scholarly opponents

Many scholars wrote about Luther's theses, some in favor of them, but most against them. Two men were most influential. The first was Dr. **John Eck**, a Dominican monk, who was an ardent defender of the papacy. He and Luther engaged in a debate at Leipzig. Although the debate was inconclusive, Eck dogged Luther for many years, both through various writings and as an agent of the pope.

Luther's other opponent of significance was **Desiderius Erasmus**,[3] the Dutch Humanist. Erasmus was troubled by the corruption in both the doctrine of the church and the practices of its clergy. Nevertheless, because of the high regard he held for the human mind, Erasmus believed that the will was able to choose good or evil, even after the Fall. For Luther, this was the crux of the problem with the Roman church—its teaching that man had some merit outside of Christ. While Erasmus was initially sympathetic to Luther, he turned

---

[2] Sam Wellman, *Frederick the Wise: Seen and Unseen Lives of Martin Luther's Protector* (St. Louis: Concordia Publishing House, 2015).

[3] Ephraim Emerton, *Desiderius Erasmus of Rotterdam* (New York: G.P. Putnam's Sons, 1899).

against him when he realized that Luther's teachings would split the church. Erasmus believed the Roman Catholic Church was the pillar of western civilization, even when it was wrong. Numerous tracts and booklets were written by Luther and Erasmus in their dispute.

"My Conscience is Bound by the Word of God"

Even though the church had tried to stop Luther though the writings of scholars[4] and with a visit by Cardinal Cajetan to pressure Luther to recant, Luther's popularity and defiance of Rome grew. Finally, Pope Leo decided it was time to excommunicate the scoundrel and have him sent to Rome for torture and/or execution. Duke Frederick the Wise, a key elector of the Holy Roman Empire,[5] was determined that his star professor would be tried in Germany and not in Italy. After much political maneuvering, Luther was invited to appear before the Imperial Diet[6] at Worms in April 1521 under a guarantee of safe conduct by Emperor Charles V.

The hearing before the diet was not intended to be a fair trial. The emperor and the Catholic Church were not interested in letting Luther make any points with the assembled members of the diet. They wanted him to recant or be executed as a heretic. Luther stalled for a day while his supporters spread the rumor of a peasant uprising if he were to be executed. Because of what had happened after Jan Hus was executed, this was a credible threat. When Luther appeared before the diet the second time, he was prepared to answer in a carefully crafted speech. He argued that he was compelled by the Scriptures to hold his positions and refused to recant unless he could be shown from the Scriptures and clear reasoning that he was wrong. This threw the diet into temporary confusion.

Mindful of the possibility of violence in the city, efforts were made to change Luther's mind in private. When these failed, he was permitted to leave

---

[4] Numerous Catholic scholars, particularly the Dominicans, began to challenge Luther's writings, emphasizing the writings of the fathers and the proclamations of the popes and councils, as the reason that Luther should be rejected.

[5] Saxony had two parts, which were ruled by dukes who were members of the same family. One duke had one of the seven electoral votes of the Holy Roman Empire, and his territory was called "electoral Saxony." The other portion was called "ducal Saxony." Wittenberg was located in the part of Saxony that determined who had the electoral vote.

[6] A "diet" was a gathering of the German noble rulers and the representatives of those cities which were recognized by the emperor as being "free," i.e., "independent," for the purpose of transacting business of interest to the parties.

for home, but after he departed, he was condemned by the part of the diet that remained. Being "placed under the ban" meant that he could be arrested or killed on sight. On the way home, he was "kidnapped" by representatives of Frederick the Wise and hidden in the Wartburg Castle. There Luther translated the New Testament of the Bible directly from Greek into German, rather than translating it from the Latin Vulgate. Then he returned to Wittenberg to begin the cleansing and restoration of the church in an orderly fashion.

Rebuilding the church

The period from the Diet of Worms (1521) to the Diet of Augsburg (1530) was the critical phase of the Reformation in terms of defining its theological orientation and building a church structure which would carry Luther's ideas to future generations. As the Lutheran reform movement spread, it attracted people who were not of the same spirit as Luther. Some of them sought personal glory by developing their own theology and seeking followers for it. Others wanted to use the Reformation to start a political revolt which would restructure German society. Some wanted to radically change the practices of the church. Luther repeatedly stressed that the sole purpose of the Reformation was to return the church to the teachings of the Scriptures.

Luther returned to Wittenberg from the Wartburg Castle when religious reform was beginning to get out of hand in Wittenberg. Lutheranism was not about destroying statues and terrorizing those who were not emotionally ready to accept changes in the church. Luther cleansed the Catholic mass of its false doctrine, changed its language to German, added hymns, and shifted the emphasis from ceremony to the sermon. He changed other practices slowly so as not to create distress among churchgoers.

Luther made it clear that the Reformation had no political agenda. Lutherans were to be good citizens, obeying the governing officials that God had placed over them. On the other hand, he also called upon the rulers to treat their subjects with respect and work for their benefit. Luther opposed those who preached revolt, such as those who fomented the Peasant War in 1525. He refused to make common cause with anyone who did not restrict their teachings to those of the Bible.

Upon surveying the congregations in Saxony, Luther and his associates determined that not only the people, but also many of the clergy did not understand even the basics of Christianity. To address this problem, he wrote two catechisms, one for the fathers to use to train their children and one for the pastors to use to train their people. The training of all pastors at colleges was emphasized so that they would be knowledgeable in the languages in which the Bible was written. Luther and a small group of scholars worked to translate the Old Testament into the German language directly from the Hebrew.

During this period Luther taught at the university, preached in the churches of Wittenberg, and wrote many books and tracts to deal with the issues which the Reformation had raised. There were plenty of opponents, scholars and would-be scholars, whose writings needed to be opposed. There were also many attracted to the Lutheran cause who needed to be properly instructed and guided onto the right path. Many rulers came to or sent delegations to Luther, seeking help in putting the Reformation's teachings into their churches. Luther's associate John Bugenhagen went to some of these territories to begin the Lutheran reform in them.

Church and State

Luther viewed the church and the state to be two separate institutions established by God. They had different responsibilities and therefore should not interfere with each other. The church was to deal with what was necessary for the salvation of people's souls, while the state was to deal with managing the political and social environment in which people lived here on Earth. Neither church nor state were to be subservient to the other.

At the time of Luther, however, the Catholic bishops who were supposed to be leading the church had abandoned this role to pursue church politics and their own ease. Luther therefore called on the princes to act as "emergency bishops" to establish good order in the church until the church itself could take over this role. This was essential for the Reformation to succeed.

Unfortunately, once the temporal rulers took control of the church organizational, they saw the advantage of making the church subservient to the state and did not let go of it. The churches became departments of the state, with rulers controlling the practices, and even the theology, of the church.

Henry VIII

Henry VIII of England (1491–1547) married Catherine of Aragon, his brother Arthur's widow. Because Arthur was only fifteen and ill when he married Catherine, she claimed that the marriage had never been consummated.

Either way, Henry[7] needed a papal dispensation to marry his brother's widow and apparently did not get it before the marriage. When Luther first arose in Germany, Henry, who was a scholar, wrote strongly against Luther, and Luther responded in kind. For his attacks on Luther, Henry was named "Defender of the Faith" by Pope Leo X.

Things did not go well for Henry in producing a male heir. He had sons by two of his mistresses, but not by his wife Catherine. While she bore sons, they all died within a few weeks. Only her daughter Mary survived to adulthood. Henry desperately needed a male heir to prevent a resumption of the War of the Roses upon his death.[8] He therefore decided that he needed to replace his wife Catherine, who was six years older than he, with a younger and more fertile woman. He chose Anne Boleyn, the sister of one of his mistresses, for the role. The pope, however, could not afford to offend Charles V, who was the nephew of Catherine and the king of Spain, as well as the Holy Roman Emperor, by granting a divorce.

In 1533 Henry VIII broke with Rome and declared himself head of the Christian church in England. This began a long struggle between the Anglican church and the Roman church for religious control of England. Henry would eventually marry six women and execute two of them for alleged adultery. Efforts to establish a united front with the Lutherans failed due to Henry's behavior and his desire to keep his church independent of alliances against Emperor Charles V.

The Swiss Reformation

Switzerland was a part of the Holy Roman Empire in the Middle Ages, and it was divided into a collection of small states called "cantons." In about 1300 these cantons started a long process of uniting to form a nation. The process was very slow because the inhabitants were separated by numerous mountains. The land was poor for farming, and many Swiss men earned at least part of their income by fighting as mercenaries in other nations' wars. This contri-

---

[7] John Bowle, *Henry VIII: A Study of Power in Action* (Boston: Little, Brown and Company, 1964).

[8] The War of the Roses was fought between two branches of the English royal family, the House of Lancaster (red rose) and the House of York (white rose) for control of the English throne. It was resolved by the establishment of the Tudor line when Henry VIII's father of Lancaster married his mother Elizabeth of York. Failure of Henry VIII to produce a male heir to the throne could have caused things to unravel again.

buted to a lack of unity because Swiss mercenaries from different cantons could be fighting on opposite sides in the same war. Swiss guards are still used today by the pope as an honor guard in Vatican City.

Huldrych Zwingli (1484–1531)[9] was born to a farm family in central Switzerland. He studied at the Universities of Vienna and Basel. He received his master-of-arts degree and was ordained a priest in 1506. He was a dedicated humanist. While he was the pastor of the church in Glarus, he came to oppose the use of Swiss troops as mercenaries in the wars of other countries because he wanted to unite all of Switzerland. Meanwhile, he studied Greek and Hebrew. In 1519 he became a priest in Zurich. There he was influenced to some extent by Erasmus and Luther as he developed his own theological model. This led to disputes in the city in 1522 and to an effort by the bishop in Constance to regain control. Nonetheless, Zwingli prevailed, and his reformation began taking on more and more radical tones. By 1526 his teachings had spread within Switzerland, causing a sharp division between his followers and the Catholics. Meanwhile, Zwingli worked to suppress the growing Anabaptist movement.[10] The Catholic Church tried to ban Zwingli's writings, and war broke out.

The war accomplished little. Zwingli thereafter felt the need to unify all the Protestant states against the Catholics. In 1529 he and his followers met with Martin Luther and his followers at Marburg in Hesse, Germany, to attempt to form an alliance. Historians have called this meeting the "Marburg Colloquy." Luther insisted there could be no military alliance without doctrinal unity. Zwingli attempted to gain an agreement by accepting fourteen of the fifteen points in contention, but Luther refused to budge on the issue of the real presence of Christ's body and blood in Holy Communion. Zwingli returned to Switzerland and filed his own statement of beliefs at the Diet of Augsburg the following year, retracting the concessions he had made to Luther. In October 1531 Zwingli was killed fighting the Catholics near Zurich when the on-again-off-again war resumed.

---

9   Jean Grob, *The Life of Ulric Zwingli (New York: Funk & Wagnalls, 1883)*.

10   The Anabaptists were against the baptism of infants, but the movement attracted anarchists who had no use for Zwingli's idea of a unified Switzerland. Most Anabaptists were not violent, but they ignored governmental institutions to the greatest extent possible. The Amish, Hutterites, and Mennonites are direct descendants of the movement.

The Augsburg Confession

Following the Diet at Worms, Emperor Charles V had had his hands full with problems outside of Germany and was not able to deal with the spread of Lutheranism. He called other diets run by his representatives, but they had not resolved the religious issue. He wanted to get the problem under control with the help of a new diet, this time at Augsburg in 1530. He asked each of the members of the diet to present a written statement of their teachings, apparently hoping to demonstrate that the teachings of the non-Catholic factions had no unity and should be dismissed as illegitimate. At the same time, the emperor needed the support of the Protestant members in his war against the Turks, so he had to tread carefully. When the leaders of the various Lutheran states and free cities arrived, Philip Melanchthon, under the watchful eye of Elector John of Saxony, the brother and successor to Frederick the Wise, and in consultation with Martin Luther who was at the Coburg Castle, [11] drew up a document stating the beliefs of the Saxons. The other Lutheran leaders agreed to accept the document that Melanchthon had drafted, thereby presenting the united front the emperor had hoped to avoid. No one, except Zwingli, presented another confession.

On June 25 the Saxon chancellor, Dr. Christian Beyer, read the German version of the document before the emperor, the diet, and a packed house. This document is now known as the "Augsburg Confession," and it is the birth certificate of the Lutheran church. It clearly states that biblical teachings are the standard of doctrine and belief. Both the German and the Latin copies of the document were presented to the emperor and his Catholic theologians.

The Catholic theologians drew up a refutation of the Augsburg Confession called the "Confutation." They read it to the diet but refused to give the Lutherans a copy. Charles V declared that the Lutherans had been refuted and gave them a deadline to return to the Catholic Church. The Lutheran party left town and began trying to recreate a copy of the Confutation from notes they had taken. Upon reaching Wittenberg, Melanchthon drew up the Lutheran response to the Confutation in which he greatly amplified what the Confession had said. This document is known as the "Apology to the Augsburg Confession."[12]

---

[11] This castle was the closest that Luther could come to Augsburg because he was an outlaw in the empire.

[12] "Apology to" in this context means "defense of."

Philip Melanchthon

Let us next consider **Philip Melanchthon** (1497–1560) and his role in the Lutheran Reformation. His original last name was Schwartzerd (black earth), which he translated into Greek, as did many other scholars of his day.[13] He gained a master's degree from the University of Heidelberg in 1516 and was brought to Wittenberg as a professor of Greek in 1518. He and Luther became friends, with Luther teaching Melanchthon theology and Melanchthon teaching Luther Greek. He soon became Luther's right-hand man. The two labored together in harmony most of the time, but Melanchthon was a humanist and more prone than Luther to introduce philosophy into his arguments. Melanchthon wrote the first dogmatics[14] textbook of Lutheranism in 1521.

Melanchthon also wrote the two great Lutheran confessions discussed above in 1530–31, but thereafter he continued to be tempted to seek concord, first with the Catholics and afterward with the Calvinists. Although he would write a third confession entitled "The Power and Primacy of the Pope," he began shifting the emphasis in his dogmatic writings to a less confrontational tone. He edited the Augsburg Confession, making it loose enough on the Sacrament of the Altar for John Calvin to sign it. Many Lutherans condemned this change, which is why many Lutheran congregations since that time declare that they subscribe to the Unaltered Augsburg Confession (UAC).

Melanchthon became a divisive force in Lutheranism after the death of Luther. During the Smalcaldic War (see chapter 10) he worked with the emperor to produce a compromise document detailing the worship practices the Lutherans would be allowed to keep. He began to teach that divine election to salvation was the result of some difference in man which caused only some to be chosen. He continued his efforts to gain unity with the southern German and Swiss Protestants, but he lost much more in the unity of Lutheranism than he gained in the unity with others. As we shall see in the next chapter, this led to Melanchthon's denouncement by many of his former colleagues.

John Calvin

John Calvin (1509–1564) was born in Noyon, France, the son of a lay church official. He was originally intended for the priesthood, but he was pre-

---

[13] Clyde L. Manschreck, *Melanchthon: The Quiet Reformer* (New York: Abingdon Press, 1958).

[14] Dogmatics is the systematic study of Christian doctrine.

cocious, so his father redirected him to the University of Orleans to study law.[15] There he became indoctrinated in humanism but also was troubled concerning his spiritual welfare. In 1532 he received his law license, and soon he took up residence in Paris. There was growing hostility between the conservative Catholic faculties at the colleges and cathedral schools in Paris and the reform-minded young professionals and students. Eventually, Calvin was forced to flee the city, and he headed to Basel in Switzerland.

During his time in Paris, Calvin had come across the works of Martin Luther and was impressed by his writings. Once in Basel, he began to study theology in earnest. In 1536 he published the first edition of his influential work *Institutes of the Christian Religion*. This work eventually grew in subsequent editions to become a four-volume dogmatics text. During the next months, he traveled to Italy and France but was forced to flee again. This time he retreated to Geneva, where he was convinced to stay. Things did not go well during this stay in Geneva, as conflict with the church organization in Bern and local politics led to Calvin being expelled from the city. Calvin headed to Strasburg to tend the French religious refugees gathering there.

In Strasburg Calvin served several churches, revised his *Institutes*, and wrote a commentary on Romans. He also married a widow with two children. When the political situation in Geneva changed in 1541, Calvin was invited back. He began a massive reform and reorganization of the church in Geneva. He taught and preached extensively, as Luther did in Wittenberg. Calvin clashed with those in Geneva who opposed his civil righteousness requirements. By 1555 Calvin's initiatives had gained thorough control of the religious and political life in the city. Geneva had effectively become a theocracy.

Like Luther, Calvin wrote numerous volumes of religious materials. He taught students, wrote hymns, and was dedicated to scholarship. He was more methodical in his habits than Luther, who liked informal table discussions and activities with his children and students. Whereas Luther looked to Scripture to interpret Scripture, Calvin looked to reason to interpret Scripture. Luther therefore embraced the irreconcilable teachings that he found in the Bible while Calvin tried to reconcile them by stressing some statements in Bible in preference to others. For Luther, the emphasis was on God's *grace*; for Calvin, the emphasis was on God's *sovereignty*.

---

[15]   William James Bouwsma, *John Calvin: A Sixteenth-Century Portrait* (New York: Oxford University Press, 1988).

10

The Struggle for Orthodoxy
AD 1546–1650

In February 1546 Martin Luther died, and his death led to major crises for the Reformation. The last half of the sixteenth century and the first half of the seventeenth century saw the Lutheran church struggle to define itself and defend itself against heretics, Calvinists, the Roman Catholic Church, and Catholic emperors. In many respects, it was the highwater mark for the Lutheran church. In other respects, it was a time when Lutheran theologians eventually lost sight of the needs of the people to whom they were ministering and set the stage for the great distresses that have troubled the Lutheran church ever since.[1]

Smalcaldic War

Almost immediately after Luther's death, the emperor finally was free to deal with the Lutherans across Germany. The members of the Smalcaldic League[2] had failed to assess their resources and act in a united fashion. With the help of Duke Maurice, the nominally Lutheran ruler of Ducal Saxony,

---

[1] Engelbrecht, *Church History*, 158–205.

Schaff, *History of the Christian Church*, Vol. 8.

Aland, *A History of Christianity*, Vol. 2, 139–156, 201–220.

F. Bente, *Historical Introduction to the Book of Concord* (Saint Louis: Concordia Publishing House, 1965).

Kolb, *Sources and Contents of The Book of Concord*.

[2] The Smalcaldic League was a defensive military alliance formed by Lutheran rulers in 1526, over Luther's objections, in response to a Catholic alliance formed in 1524.

Emperor Charles V was able to crush the Lutheran forces. Duke John Frederick of Saxony and Philip of Hesse were captured and imprisoned.

Despite his victory, the emperor had a problem. The Council of Trent had been called to deal with the issues raised by the Reformation, and it had just started meeting. The emperor wanted to impose uniformity by force, but he was uncertain what standard to use because some of the Roman Catholic teachings had never been given formal church approval. He therefore imposed, pending the conclusion of the council, what was called the Augsburg Interim for the purpose of regulating worship and other church practices in Lutheran churches. Most Lutherans vigorously opposed the Augsburg Interim, and it became clear that the emperor would not be able to enforce it. Faced with this situation, representatives of Charles V negotiated with Melanchthon and some other Lutheran theologians to establish a new interim set of instructions, called the "Leipzig Interim" (or "Leipzig Protocol"). Although never formally adopted, it caused a rift among Lutherans (see the next section).

Duke Maurice had sided with Charles V to gain the electoral vote of Saxony and other concessions. When the latter were not forthcoming, Duke Maurice changed sides and attacked and defeated the forces of the emperor. As a result, in 1555 the Peace of Augsburg was signed. It permitted the Lutheran rulers and free cities to determine the religion to be practiced within the territories that they controlled. This treaty allowed an uneasy peace to exist between Lutherans and Catholics in Germany until 1618.

Trouble among the Lutherans

The Smalcaldic War caused Lutheran theologians to fragment into three groups. Members of one group, called the Philippists, were followers of Philip Melanchthon. They were willing to compromise Luther's theology to form a union of all Protestants. They were based at the Universities of Wittenberg and Leipzig. Members of the second group were called the Gnesio-Lutherans (authentic Lutherans) and were led by Nicolaus von Amsdorf and Mathias Flacius. These theologians were based at the Universities of Jena and Magdeburg. The third group was called the "central party" and was led by Martin Chemnitz and Jacob Andreae. They were more scattered. A series of controversies arose between and within the Philippists and the Gnesio-Lutherans, the most important of which will be briefly mentioned in the following paragraphs. As indicated in each paragraph, these controversies were settled by the Formula of Concord, discussed later in this chapter.

In the **Adiaphoristic Controversy**, the Philippists defended the Leipzig Interim" which reintroduced Catholic rites into Lutheran worship services because they were only adiaphora.[3] The Gnesio-Lutherans opposed any compromise with those who taught false doctrine. Eventually, the latter were vindicated by the Formula of Concord (Article X), which declared in a time when a confession of faith is required, nothing can be conceded to be an adiaphoron.

In the **Majoristic Controversy**, George Major defended Melanchthon's remark that "good works are necessary for salvation." This error was matched by Nicolaus von Amsdorf's error that "good works are detrimental to salvation." The scriptural middle ground that good works are a natural outgrowth of faith was taken by the Formula of Concord (Article IV).

In the **Synergistic Controversy**, George Major and other Philippists held that man cooperates in his conversion. The Gnesio-Lutherans said that man contributes nothing to his conversion. The latter were vindicated by the Formula of Concord (Article II).

In the **Flacian Controversy**, Mathias Flacius maintained that original sin is the very essence of the soul of fallen man, not just a total corruption of that essence. Almost everyone else opposed Flacius, whose ideas were condemned in the Formula of Concord (Article I).

In the **Antinomian Controversy**, numerous people from the various factions argued how the Law and the Gospel applied to repentance and the sanctified life of the Christian. This was settled by the Formula of Concord (Articles V & VI).

In the **Crypto-Calvinistic Controversy**, the Philippists tried to surreptitiously insert into Lutheran dogmatics, over a period of time, Calvinistic teachings on the Lord's Supper and the majesty of the human nature of Christ. This was discovered and condemned by the rest of the Lutherans and the Formula of Concord (Articles VII & VIII).

Council of Trent

While Lutheran and Catholic military forces struggled for control of Germany, the Roman Catholic Church was getting its house in order and prepar-

---

[3] An adiaphoron (plural adiaphora) is something that is neither required nor forbidden by the Bible.

ing for a theological counteroffensive at the Council of Trent.[4] The council had been summoned to deal with the "Lutheran heresy," to codify Roman Catholic doctrine, and to eliminate abuses in the church which were causing people to flee it or ignore it. The council was called by Pope Paul III to begin in December 1545, just before the death of Martin Luther. The council had been long delayed due to a struggle between the pope and the emperor over where it would be held and what its format should be. Luther had written the "Smalcald Articles" in 1537 as his final confession of faith to be presented to the council if he were to die before the council was convened, but no Lutherans were invited to make such a presentation to the council.[5] The three popes who served during its tenure were invited, but not one of them appeared at it. The council met in three sessions: 1545–49, 1551–52 and 1562–63.

The council duly worked through the doctrines of the Roman church and made decisions on every important topic that had not been addressed previously. The work was so thorough that no new general council would be called for three hundred years. The final product was a no-nonsense approach to Catholic doctrine and to dealing with the rebelling Protestants. In addition, the church launched the Catholic (also called "Counter") Reformation, a systematic effort to protect Catholic areas from the inroads of Protestantism and to regain as much territory as possible for Catholicism. The spearhead of this effort was the Jesuit monastic order, members of which were sent to educate the children of Catholic rulers across Europe. The use of the Inquisition was also continued wherever it could be effectively carried out. Whereas twenty years earlier the momentum had been on the side of the Lutherans, it had quickly swung to the Catholics, who were finally organized and united.

The Lutheran Response to Trent

After Martin Luther, the most prominent Lutheran theologian was **Martin Chemnitz** (1522–1586), known as the "second Martin." Many feel that without Chemnitz, the Lutheran Reformation would have fallen into irreconcilable factions and most of its theology would have been lost. Born to a merchant family in Brandenburg, his early life took many twists and turns due to money

---

[4]   John W. O'Malley, *Trent: What Happened at the Council* (Cambridge, Massachusetts: The Belknap Press of Harvard University Press, 2013).

[5]   The Lutherans had long demanded a council that was not under the control of the pope. When the rules for the council were finally negotiated between the pope and the political leaders of Europe, it was clear that there would be no free discussion of Lutheran ideas.

problems brought on by his father's death, the Smalcaldic War, and the recurring plague.[6] Chemnitz attended the University of Wittenberg for only a semester before Luther died. He then moved to the University of Königsberg, from which he graduated with a master's degree. He continued to study theology and teach at Wittenberg and elsewhere in northern Germany. He was ordained to the ministry in 1554.

The Council of Trent required a Lutheran response, but the divisions among the Lutherans meant there was no one sufficiently respected and theologically prepared among the Lutheran professors to undertake the task. Chemnitz had literally trained for such a job, and between 1567 and 1573 he produced four volumes that explored the work of the council. Entitled *Examination of the Council of Trent*,[7] the four volumes looked at the entire work of the council from the viewpoint of Scripture. These volumes also evaluated it in relation to the writings of the church fathers and the historical events of the Christian church up to that point. It was not intended to be polemical but factual. Written in clear terms, it gave the divided Lutherans a standard to unite under to take on the resurgent Roman Church as it launched the Catholic Reformation. It also placed Chemnitz into a position from which he could serve as a moderator among Lutherans to establish a clear Lutheran position on all the issues that had been and were still in dispute among Lutherans.

Formula of Concord

The Peace of Augsburg had recognized only two legal religions—Roman Catholicism and Lutheranism. Rulers were told that they could choose one or the other for their territory, preferably the former. Followers of Calvin, the Anabaptists, and others had to stay underground or infiltrate the Lutheran churches to teach their doctrine. Some of the Philippists were, in reality, more Calvinistic than Lutheran (called "Crypto-Calvinists"), and this led not only to public disputes but also to covert efforts to undermine and take over portions of the Lutheran Church. Like the Catholics before the Council of Trent, the Lutherans needed a common standard to which all of them could commit. Chemnitz's response to Trent was a start, but more was required.

---

[6] J. A. O. Preus, *The Second Martin: The Life and Theology of Martin Chemnitz* (Saint Louis: Concordia Publishing House, 1994).

[7] Martin Chemnitz, *Examination of the Council of Trent*, Vols 1–4, trans. Fred Kramer (Saint Louis: Concordia Publishing House, 1971).

Various efforts to make peace among the Lutherans occurred during the 1550s and 1560s, both by the theologians directly and the theologians under the leadership of the rulers. They all failed. Then a new man began his own effort to find a peaceful resolution to some of the issues. This man was **Jacob Andreae** (1528–1590).[8] He was a leading pastor and professor in Tübingen. In his efforts to bring peace, he traveled to all the Lutheran universities and courts in Germany. In 1567 he drafted positions on five key articles—justification, good works, free will, adiaphora and the Lord's Supper—and began meeting with university faculties and princes in an attempt to gain agreement. Seemingly, progress was being made. By 1570 a meeting of Lutheran theologians from across Germany agreed on key documents that were to be part of a new set of confessions. However, the delegation from Wittenberg qualified its agreement, saying the documents were only to be accepted to the extent that they agreed with the writings of Melanchthon. There could not be unity while the Crypto-Calvinists controlled the University of Wittenberg.

Andreae's next attempt came with six sermons which were printed and sent to all the Lutheran pastors in western and central Germany in 1573. Chemnitz, with his position enhanced by his response to the Council of Trent, joined the effort, bringing other members of the central party with him. Based on Andreae's sermons, a confession called the "Swabian Concord" was drafted with eleven articles and was accepted in Swabia.[9] It was sent to Chemnitz in ducal Saxony,[10] where it was reworked into the "Swabian-Saxon Concord" and generally accepted outside of electoral Saxony.

Then suddenly, in 1574 everything changed. Duke August of electoral Saxony learned that the faculty of the University of Wittenberg, his university, was under the control of Crypto-Calvinists. The evidence was clear and unambiguous. He ousted much of the faculty, and the university was again in Lutheran hands. Following this, a document called the "Maulbronn Formula" was drafted which was considerably shorter than the Concord. Another meeting was held, this time at Torgau, where Lutheran theologians worked through the accumulated documents in great detail, making the language clear. The product of their efforts is known as the "Torgau Book."

---

[8] Ernst Henke (1875), "Andreae, Jacob," *Allgemeine Deutsche Biographie*, Vol. 1 (Leipzig: Duncker & Humblot, 1875), 436–441.

[9] Swabia is a historic region in southern Germany located to the west of Bavaria.

[10] Ducal and electoral Saxony had flipped titles after the Smalcaldic War.

By 1577 the work was done. The theologians and the rulers had looked over the final product and were satisfied. It consisted of the long Torgau Book, renamed "The Solid Declaration," with an introduction and a shorter summary called "The Epitome." It was entitled "The Formula of Concord." It was sent to Lutheran pastors, and more than eight thousand signed it, subscribing to its teachings. It was then combined with the Apostles', Nicene and Athanasian creeds, Luther's Large and Small catechisms, the Unaltered Augsburg Confession, the Apology to the Augsburg Confession, the Smalcald Articles, and the Treatise on the Power and Primacy of the Pope into a volume called the *Book of Concord*.[11] **These are the confessions of the Lutheran church.**

The Silver Age of Lutheran Orthodoxy

The Holy Scriptures are the standard to which all Lutheran teachings must conform and by which they must be judged (called *norma normans*). The documents in the Book of Concord have formed the basis of explaining Lutheran theology ever since 1580 (called *norma normata*). These latter are accepted **because** they agree with the former. Men of the sixteenth century, such as Martin Chemnitz, who helped with the drafting of the Formula of Concord, filled in key gaps and clarified earlier writings by Martin Luther and other Lutheran reformers. Yet, there was still much work to be done because the Catholic Reformation, led by the well-educated Jesuits, was beginning to press the Lutherans hard entering the seventeenth century. Moreover, the Thirty Years War was about to tear Germany apart.

To counter the influence of the Jesuits, the Lutherans developed their own form of scholasticism. New Jesuit arguments needed to be addressed, and those items which the men of the sixteenth century had not had time to discuss in adequate detail needed to be fleshed out. This period became known as the "Silver Age of Lutheran Orthodoxy." Its first and greatest theologian was **Johann Gerhard** (1582–1637). He was born in central Germany and studied at several universities. He held various posts until he became the senior professor of theology at the University in Jena in 1616. There he wrote extensively and became highly respected throughout Lutheranism. Numerous other Luth-

---

[11] Paul T. McCain, Edward A. Engelbrecht *et al.*, eds., *Concordia – The Lutheran Confessions*, 2nd ed., trans. William H. T. Dau & Gerhard F. Bente (Saint Louis: Concordia Publishing House, 2006).

eran scholars contributed writings during the era, [12] but the ongoing war limited the work through 1648. The final great theologian of the Silver Age was **Abraham Calov** (1612–86). He was born in East Prussia, educated at Königsberg, and taught at Wittenberg. He was a strong polemic writer.

Theologians of the Silver Age were thorough and were forced to be polemical by the situation vis-à-vis both the Roman Catholics and the Calvinists in Germany. They preserved the faith, improved Lutheran dogmatics, and produced much material, some of which is still in use today. On the other hand, in their effort to make sure that every possible issue was addressed, they created an orthodoxy which may have technically been correct, but which benefited the members of Lutheran congregations very little. The people were overwhelmed, and the subsequent years became a seedbed for discontent.

Further divisions in Protestantism

John Calvin was a powerful force in the Protestant community. Not only did his teachings agree more closely with human reason than did Luther's, but also Calvinism emphasized prosperity as a sign of God's favor. Calvin's teachings spread up the Rhine Basin from Switzerland to the Netherlands. Openly and covertly, people bought into a religion which often changed their behavior more than their hearts. Yet, although Calvin's teachings seem quite logical, there were things about them that made them hard for some sensitive people, particularly humanists, to accept. The most difficult sell was double predestination. This teaching maintained that while a few people had been elected to be saved, most people had been elected to be eternally damned and were programmed to live their lives to force this damnation to occur. There was bound to be pushback in some quarters to such an idea.

Jacobus Arminius (1560–1609)[13] was born in Utrecht and orphaned as a teenager. He was adopted and given the chance to attend the University of Leiden, a Calvinist stronghold. Eventually he went to Basel and Geneva and studied under Theodore Beza, Calvin's successor and head of the Calvinist movement. Once Arminius returned to Amsterdam as a preacher, he ran afoul

---

[12] Robert D. Preus, *The Theology of Post-Reformation Lutheranism*, Vol. 1 (Saint Louis: Concordia Publishing House, 1970).

Timothy Schmeling, ed., *Lives and Writing of the Great Fathers of the Lutheran Church*, (Saint Louis: Concordia Publishing House, 2016).

[13] Kaspar Brandt, *The Life of James Arminius* (London: Ward and Company, 1854).

of his colleagues for teaching that man could seek the LORD before being moved by the Gospel and the work of the Holy Spirit. This led to strong public opposition, which only grew after he became a professor at the University of Leiden in 1603. After his death, a meeting of the Dutch Reformed Church was held in Dordrecht from 1618–19.[14] It condemned the teachings of Arminius and his followers as heretical. His followers fled, many to England. More than a century later, John Wesley, founder of Methodism, would declare his dedication to the principles of Arminius. Most of today's American Evangelicals are influenced more by Arminian theology than by Calvinism.

The Thirty Years War (1618–1648)

The Thirty Years War[15] started over the issue of the succession to the Bohemian throne. It then turned into a religious war and finally into a general melee. The Bohemians were concerned that the new Catholic heir-apparent to the throne, a member of the Hapsburg family, would roll back their previously gained religious freedoms. When he sent ambassadors to act on his behalf, the angry Bohemians followed their previous custom of behavior and threw the ambassadors out of an upper-story window. This was known as "defenestration" from the Latin word *fenestra*, meaning window. The Bohemians then invited Frederick V of the Palatinate to be their king. Naturally, the Hapsburgs, the long-time rulers of the Holy Roman Empire, were enraged, and the war was on.

The Bohemians expected that all the Protestants in Europe would back them. The Protestants, however, were not united due to the Lutheran/Calvinist split. There was a particular malice toward those Calvinists who pretended to be Lutherans in order to have protection under the Treaty of Augsburg. The Catholics were also badly split, with many non-Hapsburg lands unwilling to help the overbearing Hapsburg family. In the meantime, the Turks decided to take advantage of the situation by applying pressure to the Hapsburgs. At the same time, the Netherlanders arose against their Spanish overlords. Despite this, the Hapsburgs were completely successful in the first phase of the war, subduing Bohemia and moving armies into western Germany to deal with the Netherlands. By 1625 things looked bleak for the Protestants.

---

[14] This gathering is frequently referred to as the "Synod of Dort" in English language publications.

[15] Gerhard Benecke, *Germany in the Thirty Years War* (London: St. Martin's Press, 1978).

At this critical point, the Lutheran King of Denmark entered the war. Emperor Ferdinand II turned command of his army over to Albrecht von Wallenstein, an outstanding general and virulent enemy of all things Protestant. Wallenstein's army occupied much of northern Germany and Jutland. Lacking a fleet, it was unable to defeat the Danes and the Norwegians at sea. The cost of the war caused Wallenstein to retreat south after having forced the King of Denmark to withdraw from the war in 1629.

The next phase of the war concerned who should rule in Mantua in northern Italy. Although all the candidates for the throne were Catholic, France and the empire backed different men. This led to war in Italy from 1628 to 1631. Meanwhile, in 1630 fearing the defeat and subjugation of the German Lutherans, the Lutheran King Gustavus Adolphus of Sweden brought his excellent army into the fray. He quickly overran northern Germany and came extremely close to capturing all of Germany before he was killed in battle in 1632. The Swedes continued to aid the Germans, but without their great leader, they were less effective. The Catholics rallied, and by 1635 they had defeated the Lutheran princes, who were forced to sue for peace.

The war, however, entered yet another phase. The French attacked Spain, which forced Hapsburg troops to be transferred from Germany. The Dutch also continued to give the Spanish grief in the Netherlands. The Swedes, who had reorganized their army, again marched south. Sensing territorial gains at the expense of Germany and Spain, the French also send troops into Germany. The various armies had little discipline, and many of the so-called "soldiers" were more pillagers than warriors. Murder and destruction were the rule across much of the center of Germany. More than eight million people died in the war, and Germany was in ruins.

In 1648 the Peace of Westphalia, which consisted of a group of treaties, ended the war. Numerous borders were redrawn. The Netherlands became independent of Spain. France obtained the German-speaking province of Alsace, which would become the cause of future wars. During this agonizing period, when Lutheran worship and church life was interrupted, Paul Gerhardt wrote some of his greatest hymns. Martin Rinkart, a Lutheran pastor working under unimaginably bad conditions, wrote "Now Thank We All Our God," which has become the national German hymn of thanksgiving. In the midst of their agony, Lutherans still praised the LORD.

11

The Onslaught of Human Ideas
AD 1650–1900

In the middle of the seventeenth century, life was in disarray in much of Germany. The Thirty Years War had killed a significant portion of its residents, destroyed buildings, ruined land, and left a population with little sense of morality. It also left a religious and a political struggle between Lutheranism and Calvinism for control of the non-Catholic lands in northern and central Germany. Lutheran dogmaticians of the Silver Age of Lutheran Orthodoxy produced a plethora of the theological works needed to defend the Lutheran position. Yet, deep theology was not what most people were concerned about. They wanted something that would allow them to live a peaceful and, hopefully, prosperous life, at least by the standards of the times. This was a fertile field for new religious ideas.[1]

Problems in the Pastoral Ministry

The most important point all parish pastors need to understand in every era is the need to preach from God's Word for the good of the souls in their congregations. It may be the harshness of the law or the sweetness of the gospel. It may be comfort for souls troubled by death, disease, and economic disaster. It may be warnings to those who are self-centered amid the needs of others. This requires every pastor to understand his people individually as a shepherd understands his sheep individually. Unfortunately, in the period after the Thir-

---

[1]   Engelbrecht, *Church History*, 206–323.

   Aland, *A History of Christianity*, Vol. 2, 221–330.

ty Years War, too many pastors, trained in universities where the theological battle against the Calvinists was a consuming passion, were more prepared for academic sparring than for parish service.

The theological struggle resulted in people being lambasted in sermons more often aimed at keeping them in the Lutheran church than at strengthening their faith and putting it into practice in their daily lives. The hatred and bad behavior that had become commonplace during the Thirty Years War were not adequately addressed in many Lutheran parishes. The doctrine that was taught may have been as pure as newly fallen snow, but it was over the heads of the congregation members to whom it was being preached. The people needed practical help to turn from lives filled only with cares over daily survival to lives of service to the LORD through obeying the moral law and to their neighbors through honest and helpful behavior. Some thought the need to fix this problem was so great that they were willing to overshoot the narrow Lutheran middle[2] and push people into the ditch of civil righteousness at the expense of doctrinal faithfulness.

Pietism

The founder of Pietism was **Philipp Spener** (1635–1705).[3] He was born in Alsace when it was still a part of the Holy Roman Empire. He attended the University of Strasburg and received a master's degree in 1653. For a decade he served as a tutor and toured the universities of southern Germany and Switzerland. He was highly impressed by the piety of the people of Geneva in contrast to the public immorality that he saw in so many places in Germany. He became a lecturer at Strasburg in 1663 and chief pastor of a Lutheran church in Frankfort am Main. There he fleshed out his ideas of how to bring individual piety and vigorous Christian living to the members of the Lutheran church.[4] He published his great theological works *Pia desideria* in 1675 and *Allgemeine Gottesgelehrtheit* in 1680. He got into trouble in Saxony for condemning the morals of its court but was hired in Berlin, where he found greater favor. In 1694 he was instrumental in founding the University of Halle, which would carry on his work. Despite this, he was condemned for 264 errors in

---

2   Daniel M. Deutschlander, *The Narrow Lutheran Middle* (Milwaukee: Northwestern Publishing House, 2011).

3   Johannes Wallmann, *Philipp Jakob Spener und die Anfänge des Pietismus*, 2nd ed. (Tübingen: Mohr Siebeck, 1970).

4   Robert Koester, *The Spirit of Pietism* (Milwaukee: Northwestern Publishing House, 2013).

his works by the theological faculty of the University of Wittenberg a year later.

The Pietist Movement[5] grew around six proposals that Spener set forth in *Pia desideria*. These were: 1) The Bible would best be studied in small private groups led by a pastor; 2) The laity should share in the spiritual governance of the church; 3) Christian knowledge must be coupled with visible practice to be authentic; 4) Heterodox members and unbelievers should be treated sympathetically by the church; 5) University training of pastors should emphasize devotional life; and 6) Preaching should emphasize the growth of the new man and the fruits of faith. Many orthodox Lutherans sensed in these ideas of Pietism a greater interest in improving the world than in saving souls.

Pietism emphasized good deeds by church members and the need for those seeking admittance to the church to mentally anguish over their sins and thereby prove themselves worthy of Christ by changing their lives before being baptized. When Pietism became influential in a congregation, its members often began more and more looking to their own behavior rather than the work of the Holy Spirit to build their faith. Like Luther during his days in the Augustinian monastery, church members would struggle to purify themselves from their own sins so they would feel worthy to come before God, sometimes even to pray or to take Holy Communion. Congregational norms would develop for what was held to be "good Christian living," such as abstaining from alcohol, by which fellow congregation members were judged. Sound doctrine became secondary to a holy life.

An early adherent of Spener was **August Francke** (1663–1727),[6] who was born in Lübeck and educated at the universities of Erfurt and Kiel. Francke met Spener and was impressed by him. He spent some time with him in Dresden before Spener was kicked out of Saxony, and he put Spener's teachings into practice in Leipzig. After being expelled from Leipzig, Francke went to Erfurt, from which he was soon also asked to leave. He then became a Greek professor at the University of Halle and led that institution after the death of Spener. He was especially known for his efforts to care for outcast children.

From the University of Halle, the Pietistic movement spread throughout northern and central Germany and to Scandinavia, where it effectively took

---

5   F. Ernest Stoeffler, ed., *Continental Pietism and Early American Christianity* (Grand Rapids, Michigan: Eerdmans, 1976).

6   Gary R. Sattler, *God's Glory, Neighbor's Good: A brief introduction to the life and writings of August Hermann Francke* (Chicago: Covenant Press, 1982).

over much of Lutheranism. Halle sent missionaries to the United States, India, and other places colonized by western nations. Pietism continued to influence much of the Lutheran church for the next two centuries and beyond. It even indirectly influenced John Wesley,[7] the founder of Methodism in England.

Rationalism

The notion of using reason goes back to Aristotle, who developed syllogistic logic as the basis of argumentation. Greek philosophers believed in self-evidence as a source of truth and that all truth is interconnected. This "one-truth" thesis troubled the Christian church throughout much of its history because philosophers and theologians tried to link the truths revealed in the Bible to those understood by the ancient philosophers and found in nature.

The modern "Age of Reason" or "the Enlightenment," which opened the door to Rationalism,[8] is generally held to have started with **René Descartes** (1596–1650).[9] Descartes argued that the knowledge of absolute truths, such as those of mathematics or the foundations of the sciences, could be gained from reason alone. The knowledge of the things of nature, such as the motion of the stars, the principles of physics, or the behavior of a squirrel, required the active study of nature and the use of the scientific method. Therefore, Descartes concluded that one should doubt every belief developed though sensory reality. Reason alone determined knowledge, he claimed. He is credited with making the statement, "I think, therefore I am." While Descartes predated Spener, it took time for Rationalism, i.e., the effort to explain everything through reason, to sprout and bloom from the roots of the Enlightenment. While Descartes did consider things from a religious perspective, he was so far ahead of his time that his ideas did not immediately make it into the theological schools. It is also significant that Descartes was philosophizing in France during the Thirty Years War in Germany. Lutheran theologians had more pressing problems than abstract philosophy.[10]

---

[7]   John Tedford, The Life of John Wesley (New York: Eaton & Mains, 1885).

[8]   Anthony Gottlieb, *The Dream of Enlightenment: The Rise of Modern Philosophy* (London: W. W. Norton & Company, 2016).

[9]   Desmond Clarke, *Descartes: A Biography* (Cambridge: Cambridge University Press, 2006).

[10] Other early Rationalists were Baruch Spinoza and Gottfried Leibniz.

Rationalism and Christianity

Rationalism moved from the realm of philosophy into theology in waves over the next two centuries. Theologians tried to apply reason to Christian teachings, which quickly disconnected the teachings from the Bible. By 1696 English philosopher and deist[11] **John Toland** (1670–1722)[12] claimed, "There is nothing in the Gospels contrary to reason, nor above it." Other English philosophers began claiming that the Old Testament prophecies had never been fulfilled and that the New Testament miracles were beyond belief. **Matthew Tindal** (1657–1733)[13] argued that the only essential part of Christianity was its ethics because they appealed to natural reason.

During the eighteenth century, other voices arose favoring a rational foundation for Christianity. In France, **Voltaire** (1694–1778)[14] thought that a belief in God was acceptable, but a belief in divine revelation irrational. He ridiculed the Christian idea of salvation. In East Prussia, **Immanuel Kant** (1724–1804)[15] argued that human perception defines the laws of nature and that reason is the source of morality. He called his concept "Transcendental Idealism," and he propounded it in his famous book *The Critique of Pure Reason*. He argued that pure reason is "flawed when it goes beyond its limits and claims to know those things that are beyond the realm of experience, such as the existence of God." Kant therefore concluded that both reason and experience are necessary for human knowledge.

The effects of Rationalism on the Christian church in general were devastating. As the ideas of the philosophers infiltrated the religion departments of universities, the training of pastors significantly changed. Views of God more and more featured man in control and God tagging along. Church members were told to rationalize what they found in the Bible so biblical teachings would benefit their material and intellectual lives. Rationalism taught that everything could be explained by brilliant men like Isaac Newton, and the rest of mankind could benefit from following their lead. The mind was supreme, and God needed to be understood in terms of man's intellectual accomplishments. This type of preaching emptied Christian churches. It gave no comfort

---

11 A deist believes that God created the universe and then abandoned it to run itself.
12 Alan Harrison, *John Toland (1670–1722)* (Baile Átha Cliath: Coiscéim, 1994).
13 Stephen Lalor, *Matthew Tindal, Freethinker: An Eighteenth-century Assault on Religion* (London: Continuum International Publishing Group Ltd., 2006).
14 Ira O. Wade, *Studies on Voltaire* (New York: Russell & Russell, 1967).
15 C. D. Broad, *Kant: An Introduction* (Cambridge: Cambridge University Press, 1978).

to the troubled soul and provided no way of salvation when the body returned to the dust. The resistance to these ideas in Lutheran churches varied, depending upon which university the pastor to a particular congregation came from. Members in smaller, more rural churches were less affected than those in major cities because rural congregations tended not to attract pastors from the more prestigious schools in which Rationalism was rampant.

Rationalism and Colonialism

A lingering negative aspect of Rationalism is that it was used to justify imperialism. Because European nations were able to build better weapons of war and ocean-going ships, their citizens thought they had God-given enlightened minds which were superior to those of other peoples. Therefore, it was only rational that they should rule over other peoples. They should take those things that were necessary for their own prosperity, such as land, minerals, timber, etc., which other peoples were underusing. From the sixteenth century and until the time of Winston Churchill, European dominance over other cultures was a tenet of Rationalist thought. Certainly, it was not the only influence driving colonialism, but it was a significant factor.

Where lands were temperate in climate and not heavily populated, European settlers seized everything in sight. This was true in North America, parts of South America, Australia, and New Zealand. In other places they merely established a dominant presence so as to exploit both natural resources and "cheap" local labor. The nations in Europe sought the best "unclaimed" lands for themselves and sometimes fought each other for them, such as in the French and Indian War of 1763. Where Europeans settled in large numbers, they expected they would have the same rights as people had in their native countries. This did not always happen, and the settlers sometimes revolted against their mother countries to demand such rights. The most notable of these rebellions was that of the colonies of Great Britain in North America in 1776, which led to the formation of the United States. The Declaration of Independence is an example of the Rationalism in vogue at the time. The fathers of the American Revolution for the most part were deists, not Christians.

Where European colonists were in the minority, they ruled with the backing of the military and naval forces of their home countries. Non-Europeans had few, if any, rights, and some were treated little better than slaves. This was justified as part of the "white man's burden" to manage the world, in the name of the Lord God, for the benefit of all and to train the natives to adopt superior European ways. These ideas did not end until the middle of the twentieth century. Lutherans were less affected by the problems of colonization than other Christians because Lutheran countries were not as likely to plant colonies as were those countries which were Reformed or Catholic.

Rationalism and the Industrial Revolution

The Industrial Revolution began when clever people found ways to do things more efficiently.[16] It was a slow process because it often involved a chain of inventions occurring in a specific order to reach a point where a significant change could occur. The manufacture of textiles, for example, was an industry where the accumulation of many small changes finally produced major improvements through economies of scale. To the promoters of the glories of the Enlightenment, this use of the mind to ease the hard work otherwise required of the hands was visible proof of the rightness of their cause.

Industrialization was a "snowballing" type of process. Getting the process started required people having the necessary time to spend thinking up and testing innovations. When people were using all their waking hours simply to earn what was necessary to feed and clothe themselves, little progress could be made. When the lords of the land were more interested in warring and enjoying their privileged life than in the plight of their subjects, one generation faded into the next without noticeable change. It was only when people were willing to create free time for those with curious minds and able hands to work on something new that inventions began to appear. The universities of the seventeenth and eighteenth centuries were where the ideas of change began, and merchants looking for an advantage were often the financers of beneficial changes. The Enlightenment brought these people together to form "the invisible hand," the force that **Adam Smith** in his book *The Wealth of Nations* (1776)[17] declared would drive practical economics in the right direction without the necessity of guidance by the state.

Before the Industrial Revolution, people had looked to God to sustain and prosper their work, which was often dependent on favorable weather. As the

---

[16] W. Bernard Carlson, *Understanding the Inventions That Changed the World* (Chantilly, Virginia: The Great Courses Teaching Company, 2013).

[17] F. Glahe, *Adam Smith and the Wealth of Nations: 1776–1976* (Boulder, Colorado: University Press of Colorado, 1977).

Industrial Revolution produced more material goods and a higher standard of living, people began looking more to themselves and less to God. They rationalized that they did not need God's help when they could help themselves. In the same way, Rationalism still suppresses people's dependence on God today. In addition, industrialization caused people to move from rural areas, where Lutheran pastors often held a dominant position in their communities, to cities, where seductive voices offering alterative views of truth and morality were available to draw people away from the church.

Theological Liberalism

Not all church leaders were willing to so readily toss God onto the slag heap of history. Some looked at the Scriptures and thought there was something worth saving. Man had more than a mind, they claimed; he also had a heart, and both needed to be involved in a balanced life. This led to a movement called "Theological Liberalism." The Liberalists thought that if they could remove the "husk" of cultural specificity overlaying the biblical truths, they could reveal God's message and repackage it into a form that would be powerful and would improve the world for all mankind.

Friedrich Schleiermacher (1768–1834)[18] was the founder of this movement. His plan was to reconcile the human brilliance that had been born in the Renaissance and matured during the Enlightenment with traditional Protestant Christianity. To accomplish this, he proposed using "higher criticism." Lutherans previously had understood the Bible by the historical grammatical method, where the historical and textual contexts were used along with the grammatical sense of the words to permit a consistent and accurate interpretation.[19] Schleiermacher rejected this traditional way in favor of a method in which the Bible was read like other ancient books, namely, in terms of the myths and other cultural artifacts that shaped the underlying truth. These truths needed to be conveyed to people of other cultural traditions. To properly interpret the Bible, therefore, it was necessary to strip away the cultural baggage, so the hidden truth could be revealed.

---

[18]   Richard Crouter, *Friedrich Schleiermacher: Between Enlightenment and Romanticism* (Cambridge: Cambridge University Press: 2008).
[19]   Arthur A. Eggert, *Simply Lutheran* (Milwaukee: Northwestern Publishing House, 2020).

Albrecht Ritschl (1822–1889)[20] was a dogmatist who built on Schleiermacher's ideas. In his theology, faith needed to be set in the context of experiences which were beyond the scope of reason. Faith, he said, came not from facts but from value judgments. This allowed him to dismiss the plain textual meaning of the Scriptures in favor of a mystical meaning that, he asserted, was the real message of God. For example, Jesus's divinity, he claimed, should be understood in terms of a revelation to the community that Christ served rather than as a historically demonstrable truth. He taught that the Christian message was a community-building message, and it was to be spread for the purpose of including others in the community.

Charles Darwin's[21] books on the evolution of plants and animals, particularly *On the Origin of Species*, had a major impact on the development of Theological Liberalism. Darwin's ideas were not completely new, having been speculated about in intellectual circles for some time. Darwin, however, had real evidence to present and a theory, although yet incompletely formed, that would explain how living things changed over long periods of time. Obviously, this new evidence impacted the age of the earth because the earth's age needed to accommodate sufficient time for such evolution to occur. Liberalist theologians saw this development in science as a validation of their approach to the Bible because standard methods of interpretation could not handle the new developments in modern scientific studies.

Walter Rauschenbusch (1861–1918)[22] was an American Baptist theologian who taught at Rochester Theological Seminary. Unlike the Southern Baptists, who are known for their insistence on traditional biblical interpretation, American Baptists are much closer to the mainline Protestant churches, except in the doctrine of Baptism. Like August Francke, Rauschenbusch was appalled by the ill treatment the poor experienced, and he felt that alleviating their poverty should be a major function of the Christian church. He was instrumental in the development of the "social gospel," which pointed the church's activities away from the direct proclamation of the gospel of Jesus

---

[20] David Livingstone Mueller, *An Introduction to the Theology of Albrecht Ritschl* (London: Westminster Press, 1969).
[21] Adrian Desmond & James Morre, *Darwin* (London: Michael Joseph, Penguin Group, 1991).
[22] Paul M. Minus, *Walter Rauschenbusch: American Reformer* (New York: Macmillan Publishing Company, 1988).

Christ. Instead, it used a social concern for others as a means of demonstrating God's love in action and, in theory, thereby attracting people to become part of the Christian mission of showing Jesus's love. It was a form of synergism in which works and faith became intermingled in the spiritual mindset of the Christian. It naturally followed that Rauschenbusch saw political activity as a legitimate function of the church in carrying out its responsibility to help the underprivileged.

Theological Liberalism emphasized "community Christianity" rather than "personal Christianity." It anticipated that by working together the members of the Christian church could eventually transform the world into a paradise. Mankind would not have to wait until death for a divine heaven in a different plane of existence. This was completely different from what the Scriptures teach, but numerous Lutherans became involved in this movement. Liberalist Christianity was quite popular in Europe, where people hoped it could help heal the long-standing divisions on the continent. It experienced a crushing blow with the destructiveness of World War I and the subsequent Spanish Flu. Both events showed that neither man nor God was committed to turning the world into a utopia where mankind would live free of mental anguish and physical need. This world exists under the curse of sin. God may allow people to make economic or social improvements, but he will not allow people to become too proud of their accomplishments. The ideas of Liberalist Christianity were to be revived after World War II, but in a very different context.

The assaults on biblical teachings by Pietism, Rationalism, and Theological Liberalism did considerable damage to the Christian church and snuffed out the faith of many individual Christians. Yet, the changes in the political and the religious worlds in this period were no longer so closely linked to each other as they had been before the middle of the seventeenth century. With a greater degree of religious freedom, conflicts that did exist between the church and state became more localized. The "wars and rumors of wars" of Matthew 24:6 persisted, and people continued to struggle to gain power in governmental and church bodies. Nevertheless, what happened in one nation did not, in general, affect what was happening in the churches of another. The arrival of Napoleon would again bring religion and secular politics into conflict on a large scale, as we will see in the next chapter.

12

The Confessional Reawakening
AD 1800–1918

By the beginning of the nineteenth century, the onslaught of human ideas about the Christian message had had its effect upon the Lutheran church in numerous ways. Some of these were directly through what was preached from the pulpit. Some were indirectly through the changing nature of society. Some were through the traditional work of Satan, who is always inciting people to rebel against the teachings of the LORD. Yet, the LORD did not abandon his struggling Lutheran flock, even if some of its leaders did.[1]

Historic Lutheranism

Martin Luther established a gestalt for what future Lutherans were to be. A Lutheran was someone who learned his theology from the Scriptures and who had complete confidence in the LORD. Lutherans did not inquisitively look beyond the Bible to find explanations for how God dealt with mankind. If the Bible said it, for Lutherans, that settled it (see the contrast with Arminianism in chapter 14). They did not seek outside validation, and they knew the Bible was true whether they believed it or not. They also were certain that

---

[1] Engelbrecht, *Church History*, 206–323.

Aland, *A History of Christianity*, Vol. 2, 331–398.

John M. Brenner, *The Election Controversy Among Lutherans in the Twentieth Century: An Examination of the Underlying Problems* (Milwaukee: epublications.marquette.edu/dissertations_mu/204, 2012), 7–185.

the LORD would take care of them in the manner which he knew would be best for them.

It is natural that Lutheranism was strong in rural areas, particularly among farmers. Farmers knew that God controlled nature. They realized they were dependent on the weather which God gave them and on his care for their lives and the lives of their farm animals. They saw very clearly how life and death were in the hands of the LORD. As human ideas and inventions affected people's lives more and more, people migrated from the countryside, where it seemed to them that God was dominant, to the cities, where it seemed to them that men were dominant. As the percentage of Lutherans who lived in the cities grew, more were exposed to, and pressured to accept, the ideas of the Calvinists and of the Rationalists. These ideas seemed more in tune with the changing world.

Worse yet, numerous Lutheran professors had become disconnected from the Lutheran congregation members for whom they should have been training pastors. This left the Lutheran laity open to the encroachment of non-biblical ideas. Too many pastors were only nominally tending their sheep, without giving due attention to what was troubling the sheep in a period which saw rapid technological and economic growth. Events were about to shatter this complacency among Lutheran leaders. The Lutheran church was about to be awakened by men who were committed to the ideas of Luther.

The Prussian Union

The Peace of Westphalia allowed rulers to determine which religion or religions could be practiced in the lands they controlled. Most of the non-Catholic lands had been Lutheran in the sixteenth century. Where the princes, dukes, and other lords subsequently converted to Calvinism, they were often faced with an entrenched Lutheran population. They therefore permitted both churches to exist but established separate imperial oversight committees. In a few Protestant lands, Roman Catholics churches were also permitted. The existence of both Calvinist and Lutheran churches in the same cities led to pastors of each church sharply condemning the teachings of the other church. This caused strife and disunity within the various cities and states of Germany, and it was not to the liking of the rulers. Where the polemics were particularly strong, such as in Berlin, the government forbade doctrinal attacks in sermons and sent agents into the churches to enforce these edicts.

After the Reformation, the Lutheran churches were supported by funds from various sources. One source of financing was collections from the members of the congregations in established cities and in independent villages. If a church stood on land owned by a lord, then the lord might provide some support for the church to minister to his serfs and peasants. Kings, princes, and dukes might provide funds for churches that were part of their universities. Rich people in congregations might give gifts for congregational functions to which they attached particular significance. Some funds might be gathered from renting church lands for agricultural purposes, although this greatly decreased after most surplus church property was confiscated by rulers following the Reformation. Although the various levels of governments tried to regulate the churches as much as they could, their hands were weakened by the lack of complete financial control of the churches.

The situation changed greatly when Napoleon conquered much of Germany. Napoleon did not want the churches to have an independent financial base. He wanted them dependent upon the state so that the state could better control them. He therefore forbade churches from collecting money from their members and put the churches on state subsidy. After Napoleon was defeated, rulers across Europe saw the wisdom, at least from their point of view, of making the churches departments of the state. Most church leaders accepted the idea because it made the job of keeping their congregations financially viable easier. Church leaders, however, soon learned that with government money came at least some degree of government control. Despite this unwanted interference, churches today in many European countries are still supported by tax money.

The 300th anniversary of the Lutheran Reformation occurred in 1817. Calvinist King Frederick Wilhelm III of Prussia became upset with the continuing division between the Lutheran and Calvinist (Reformed) parts of the Protestant church.[2] It was a personal matter with him because he and his Lutheran wife could not attend Holy Communion together. He therefore declared an administrative union of the church. The churches could retain their doctrine, but they were ordered to work out a compromise that would permit members of both churches to take the Sacrament of the Altar together and that would allow the churches to act functionally as one organization. With the churches

---

[2] Robert M. Bigler, *The Politics of German Protestantism: The Rise of the Protestant Church Elite in Prussia, 1815–1848* (Berkeley: University of California Press, 1972).

being financially supported by the state, most congregations of both church bodies agreed to the arrangement, which was accomplished through a compromise liturgy. Lutherans, weakened by the teachings of Pietism and Rationalism, were not able to put up a united front against this absurdity. The words of institution for Holy Communion were changed so they could be understood either in the Lutheran or Calvinist way. Universities began training pastors so that they could work under either set of doctrines. Prussia did not control all of Germany at the time, but other Protestant states saw this approach as a solution to a continuing problem and followed Prussia's lead. The new church was called "The Church of the Prussian Union."

The "Old Lutherans" Underground

Although the Lutheran church in German territories had been weakened by Pietism and Rationalism during the previous two centuries, there were still many Lutherans who did resist the edict of Frederick Wilhelm III. Some congregations tried to follow the old practices but had government agents seize their pastors and replace them with pastors who would comply with the edict. Some Lutherans held unauthorized services in open spaces or in people's houses. Other Lutherans moved across the borders into states that did not enforce this law. Some fled to America or Australia.

Those who resisted the Prussian Union were referred to as "Old Lutherans."[3] As the opportunity presented itself, they formed congregations outside of the official government church. Because they received no government subsidy, they were called "free" churches. As Prussia took over more of Germany, particularly more Roman Catholic areas, it became harder to enforce the edict, and more free churches were formed. King Frederick Wilhelm IV, a rationalist, formally permitted free churches after 1845. While the Prussian Union, under the name "*Evangelisch*," remains the official Protestant church of Germany, Lutheran free churches also continue to survive there today.

Lutheranism in the New World

Lutheran settlers began arriving in North America from Scandinavia, the Netherlands, and Germany. The first settlements were along the Hudson River

---

[3] Christopher Clark, "Confessional Policy and the Limits of State Action: Frederick William III and the Prussian Church Union 1817–40," *Historical Journal* 39.04 (1996), 985–1004.

in the 1620s. The first Lutheran congregation in this region was formed in 1648. Lutherans from Sweden formed a congregation in the temporary Swedish colony of New Sweden in the Delaware River Valley in 1638 and built the first Lutheran church in America in 1646. These congregations remained small until an influx of Lutherans arrived from the Palatinate in the early eighteenth century, caused in part by conflicts with Reformed rulers in that area. Lutherans driven out of Salzburg in Austria settled in Georgia in 1734, bringing Lutheranism to the South. Lutherans also spread from Virginia into North Carolina.

The first effort to form groups of churches occurred under the leadership of **Heinrich Melchior Mühlenberg** (1711–87),[4] who is regarded as the "Father of American Lutheranism." He traveled tirelessly throughout the colonies to reach scattered Lutherans and bring them together. He founded the Pennsylvania Ministerium[5] in 1748. His work also led to the formation of the New York Ministerium in 1786 and the North Carolina Synod in 1803. The major goals of these synods were to obtain doctrinal unity and to train pastors. The pastors involved in establishing colonial congregations were of diverse theological backgrounds. Some only accepted the Augsburg Confession and not the whole *Book of Concord*. Some were heavily influenced by Pietism, while others were more orthodox. All the synods were very small.

The General Synod was organized in 1820 as a federation of the three synods mentioned in the previous paragraph and the Synod of Maryland and Virginia. The membership of the group was unstable because it did not have a common doctrinal standard. Whether a doctrinal standard should be enforced was a recurring issue. Some members were willing to compromise with the Reformed churches, and some were not. Some wanted a hierarchical structure, and some did not. In response to the laxity of the General Synod, ten regional synods formed the General Council in 1867. This new organization placed emphasis on subscription to the Lutheran Confessions and adopted the Akron-Galesburg Rule, which stated that Lutheran pulpits were for Lutheran pastors and Lutheran altars were for Lutheran communicants. Despite these noble intentions, there was little enforcement of the General Council's decisions, and methods of resolving new issues were lacking.

---

[4]   William J. Mann, *Life and Times of Henry Melchior Muhlenberg* (Philadelphia: G.W. Frederick. 1888).

[5]   A ministerium is like a synod but does not have lay participation in its governance.

The Saxon Migration – The Confessional Lutheran Influx

While the Old Lutherans struggled against the Prussian Union, a younger group of Lutherans chaffed under the Rationalism that was dominating Lutheran pulpits in Saxony. A Lutheran pastor in Dresden named **Martin Stephan** (1777–1846) began preaching a confessional Lutheran message in 1830. Members from other Lutheran congregations were attracted by his message to join his church, resulting in concern among their former pastors. A small number of pastors and seminary students, along with a group of laypeople, escaped from Saxony, which opposed their intent to emigrate to America. A group of 707 people reached Bremen and, in 1838, sailed on five ships for New Orleans. It then traveled up the Mississippi River to St. Louis. Most of the group settled south of St. Louis in Perry County, Missouri. At the prompting of other Midwestern Lutherans, they founded the Missouri Synod in 1847. One of the ships was lost in the Atlantic crossing, the one which contained the bulk of the liturgical vestments and paraments.

Problems developed soon after the Saxon Lutherans arrived in Perry County. Pastor Stephan became dictatorial in temporal matters. He was removed from his leadership position and expelled from the community because of accusations of sexual impropriety. There was then a division among the settlers, with some members deciding to return to Europe, and the rest following Pastor **C.F.W. Walther** (1811–87).[6] Walther was a workhorse. He was the pastor of Trinity Lutheran Church in St. Louis, president of the Missouri Synod,[7] president of Concordia Lutheran Seminary in St. Louis, and editor of *Der Lutheraner* and *Lehre und Wehre*.[8] He was also the Missouri Synod's leading theologian. Under his leadership the Synodical Conference was formed with other Lutheran synods that met Walther's strict standard of orthodoxy.

Indeed, the influx of Lutherans from Europe led to the formation of many small synods. They were primarily divided by state, if the Lutherans came from Germany, and by nationality, if they came from elsewhere. Every midwestern state had at least one German Lutheran synod. The most enduring of

---

[6]   August Robert Suelflow, *Servant of the Word: The Life and Ministry of C.F.W. Walther* (Saint Louis: Concordia Publishing House, 2001).

[7]   Walter A. Baepler, *A Century of Grace: A History of the Missouri Synod, 1847–1947* (Saint Louis: Concordia Publishing House, 1947).

[8]   *Lehre und Wehre* means "teach and defend."

these outside Missouri was the Wisconsin Synod. It began as a somewhat unionistic assemblage because of its sponsorship by the Prussian Union missionary societies, but it came to be a bastion of confessional Lutheranism under the theological leadership of **Adolf Hoenecke** (1835–1908).[9] In fact, the orthodoxy of all the Lutheran synods was affected by the missionary societies that funded them and supplied them with pastors. Those societies associated with the University of Halle were particularly active in sending missionaries to the United States. They were both Pietistic and under the control of the Prussian Union. The pastors they sent were instructed to be ready to serve either Lutheran or Reformed congregations. This meant many had a weak loyalty to the Lutheran Confessions. There was a need for the "Lutheran" synods to examine their theology, sort out who was genuinely Lutheran, and establish their own seminaries to preserve their internal doctrinal unity. Some of them became members of the General Synod, while others became members of the General Council, but the laxity in these groups sometimes caused synods to split over the desirability of such membership.

The Synodical Conference

The difficulties within the General Synod and the General Council led several midwestern Lutheran synods to begin discussions on forming a firmly confessional Lutheran organization. In 1872 the Missouri, Ohio, Wisconsin, Illinois, Minnesota, and Norwegian synods agreed that they held to the same doctrine and practice, and therefore they could work together in all matters of the ministry. They formed an organization called the Synodical Conference. In 1880 the Illinois Synod merged into the Missouri Synod and became its Illinois District.[10]

The existence of numerous small synods established within the boundary of one state, but sometimes reaching into neighboring states, posed a problem for the future of the Synodical Conference. Church discipline and orderly church programs would be hard to maintain if people could flow among the synods at will. It was decided to work toward three larger synods, the Ohio Synod in the east, the Missouri Synod in the southwest and the Wisconsin

---

[9] A. P. Voss, ed., *Continuing in His Word* (Milwaukee: Northwestern Publishing House, 1951), 19–26.

[10] During their history, the Lutheran synods have frequently changed their names. This has been due to mergers, splits, simplifications, and efforts to enhance their image. The most common names by which the synods have been known are used in this book.

Synod in the north central region. Gradually, some smaller state synods did merge into these three bodies, but doctrinal issues prevented this plan from being completed.

The old question that had led Melanchthon astray, namely, of reconciling universal grace with election reappeared in a new form, "Did God elect people for salvation 'into faith' or 'in view of faith' (*intuitu fidei*)?" In 1877 Walther presented a paper advocating the former position. The Missouri and Wisconsin synods closed ranks behind Walther over the next several years, but Matthias Loy, the president and leading theologian of the Ohio Synod, broke with Walther and insisted that people were elected because God foresaw that they would believe. This was called the "Election Controversy." In 1881, the Ohio Synod left the Synodical Conference. The Norwegian Synod fragmented as a result of the controversy and also withdrew from the Conference.

In 1890 the English Lutheran Synod of Missouri joined the Synodical Conference and eventually merged into the Missouri Synod. The Michigan Synod joined the Conference in 1892, and it soon merged with the Wisconsin and Minnesota synods into a joint synod. This synod eventually shortened its name once more to the "Wisconsin Synod."

The Scandinavian Influx

The lack of quality farmland was a continuing difficulty for the people of Norway and Sweden. As the populations of these countries grew, there was little alternative for people but to emigrate to some place where they could grow sufficient food. About 25% of the Norwegian population and 20% of the Swedish population came to America. People also came to America from Denmark, Iceland, Finland, and the Baltic states, but the percentage of their populations that emigrated was much smaller because the shortage of land in those countries was not so acute. While immigrants from these lands were nominally Lutheran, most of their churches had accepted only the Augsburg Confession and Luther's Small Catechism but not the rest of the *Book of Concord*. Many came from churches that had been heavily influenced by Pietism. On the other hand, they had not had the Prussian Union imposed on them, so they were less eager to seek non-Lutheran fellowship and/or mergers.

The major problem Scandinavians brought with them was their languages. While the German Lutherans were united by language, even when they were not completely united by doctrine, the Lutherans from other countries were often divided by both language and doctrine from the rest of the Lutherans in America. Virtually all immigrant Lutheran pastors spoke, or at least could read, German because they needed to be able to read Luther's writings. This, however, was not true of the laypeople. The Finns formed the Suomi Synod. The Swedes formed the Augustana Synod. The Norwegians were divided among three synods based on which of three great Norwegian pastors they followed. Those from the Baltic states were generally absorbed into German congregations.

Further Efforts at Seeking Lutheran Unity

From the middle of the 1880s until World War I, the various Lutheran synods in the United States attempted to find ways of becoming more effective. They needed to guarantee themselves a reliable source of theologically sound pastors. They wanted to increase their membership numbers and the area of the country which they served. The most direct route to accomplish these goals was through associations of synods that shared the same view of Lutheran teachings and by organic mergers of the smaller synods into larger ones. The Lutheran landscape in America was so splintered it resembled Germany in the Middle Ages. Faced with this disarray, Lutherans sought ways of finding greater unity. The General Synod, the General Council and the Synodical Conference were all efforts to gather like-minded Lutherans into larger bodies, but doctrinal disagreements often retarded progress, with the organizations both growing and shrinking as member synods changed allegiances. Two major efforts within this collection of Lutheran synods are worth noting.

One effort involved the German synods that were not comfortable with the laxity of the General Council but that also found the Synodical Conference to be too rigid. The chief of these was the Ohio Synod, which left the Conference in 1881, as previously mentioned. Although it had significant theological differences with the less-orthodox Iowa Synod, it formed an alliance with it out of the need to extend its base westward. The Buffalo Synod, a group formed by Old Lutheran immigrants from Prussia, had initially been excluded from other Lutheran groups due to the hierarchical view of the ministry held by its leader Johannes Grabau. Over time, the group's membership was pared through theological disputes. Gradually, it was drawn into the orbit of the Ohio Synod. The Ohio, Iowa and Buffalo synods developed a working relationship that drew them closer together, but they did not merge to form the American Lutheran Church until 1930.

The Norwegian Synod had lost a third of its members during the Election Controversy. By the 1890s Norwegians were organized among three synods, each having formed through a quite different route. These were the Norwegian Synod, the United Norwegian Synod, and the Hauge Synod. These three synods had significant theological differences, but their members were highly interrelated. Different church memberships made family gatherings difficult and often caused strife within Norwegian communities.

To improve relations within their communities, the three church bodies agreed to work together to prepare a new Norwegian hymnal which they all would use. This was a strategic blunder for the more orthodox Norwegian Synod. The project attracted those who were more interested in Norwegian Lutheran unity than in addressing the divisive doctrinal issues. Once the hymnal was completed and the leadership of the Norwegian Synod had turned over, the three groups agreed to merge to form a new Norwegian synod in 1917, officially called the Norwegian Lutheran Church in America. A small group of pastors and congregations in the Norwegian Synod declined to join the merger due to the unresolved doctrinal disagreements. They formed the Norwegian Synod of the American Evangelical Lutheran Church in 1918 and joined the Synodical Conference in 1920.

The last third of the nineteenth century and the first decade of the twentieth century were a time of immense national growth in the United States. Many immigrants arrived to take advantage of new opportunities in America. The quality of Lutheranism declined in much of Europe due to Pietism, Rationalism, Theological Liberalism, and the Prussian Union. In America, Lutheran churches were growing with new members coming from overseas and with well-trained clergymen. Confessional Lutheranism in the form of the Synodical Conference had defined itself, and it was spreading with the help of the railroads and religious publications. The Missouri Synod benefitted more than the rest of the confessional Lutheran churches due to high lay involvement in its ministries and aggressive evangelism programs. Church attendance was strong, and many families had regular home devotions. The future indeed looked bright in 1910.

13

Unity versus Confessionalism
AD 1918–2020

Between 1890 and 1920, the world of Lutheranism changed radically, and it would continue to change throughout the twentieth century. No one at the beginning of this thirty-year period could have imagined the extent to which the political, scientific, economic, demographic, and religious landscapes of the world would evolve by its end. This was an era of general optimism, and many people wondered how much better things could get.[1]

Societal Changes in the Early Twentieth Century

One major event affecting the Lutheran church, although most members did not realize it at the time, was the official disappearance of the western frontier in the United States in 1890. With the "open spaces" filled, there was less reason for immigrants to come to America from Germany and Scandinavia. Moreover, the German Empire had become prosperous, and its laws had been liberalized, so poverty and religious oppression were no longer driving Lutherans to emigrate. Lutheran churches in America, which had grown from the continual influx of immigrants, were progressively needing to serve a population that was becoming more American in behavior and language. Although there were hundreds of foreign language newspapers printed in the United States at the beginning of the twentieth century and although Milwau-

---

[1] Engelbrecht, *Church History*, 206–364.

Aland, *A History of Christianity*, Vol. 2, 399–497.

Brenner, *The Election Controversy*, 186–276.

kee was still a stop on the German theater circuit, the language change to English among immigrants was accelerating.

The scientific world was suddenly transformed in 1905 when German scientist Albert Einstein published four mindset-changing papers in the field of physics.[2] Critical difficulties in explaining natural phenomena by Newtonian physics had been piling up by the end of the nineteenth century. After 1905, however, dramatic gains were made in numerous areas of physics. While few people understood physics, everyone understood and was amazed by the Wright brothers' first airplane flight. Thomas Edison's laboratory continued to churn out inventions that improved the lives of the common people. Henry Ford began producing cars on an assembly line, making them affordable for the ordinary person. These developments set the stage for the technical revolution of the 20th century. They also brought strong pressure on Christianity to explain its relevance in an era of human ingenuity.

At this time when the world seemed to be going along well materially, suddenly World War I occurred. It devastated France and Western Russia. It left millions dead. It was followed by the Spanish Flu which left millions more dead. The war caused a redrawing of European borders, leaving Europe even more unstable than before the war. For the Lutheran churches in America, World War I produced a radical environmental change. The government became hostile to foreign-language-speaking people, foreign language newspapers, and foreign-language worship services. People who could not speak English were at a terrible disadvantage and were regarded with suspicion. Everyone tried to learn English rapidly. Most foreign language newspapers and magazines went out of business. Numerous Lutheran churches moved to worshiping only in English, despite the hardship it caused for some members. In many Lutheran synods, English language religious materials were in short supply. Materials from the Episcopal and Methodist churches often ended up in Lutheran homes. Lutheran families that had long practiced daily devotions in their mother tongue found their children no longer being able to participate. Within a single generation the number of families holding daily devotions rapidly declined. Many people felt they had to choose between Lutheranism and Americanism, and they chose the latter.

---

[2]   Richard Wolfson, *Einstein's Relativity and the Quantum Revolution: Modern Physics for Non-Scientists*, 2nd ed. (Chantilly, Virginia: The Great Courses Teaching Company, 2000).

Changes in Lutheranism after World War I

Soon after arriving in the United States, Lutherans had formed synods based on language, place of European origin, and location of current residence (see previous chapter). These synods were scattered and lacked cohesiveness. Efforts to form larger Lutheran groups were frustrated by doctrinal differences, by organizational differences, by language differences, and by personality differences among church leaders. World War I drove the divided Lutherans to seek common ground. The pressure everyone felt to learn English removed one of the dividing factors. Another factor disappeared as the founders of the various synods and their sons died and were replaced by those who felt less of a stake in preserving the "old cultural norms." Also, while numerous Lutheran synods existed, there were considerably fewer Lutheran seminaries. Smaller synods increasingly had to rely on the seminaries of other synods to train their pastors. Men got to know each other in such schools, and this facilitated and even encouraged the numerous organizational mergers which dramatically shrank the number of Lutheran synods over the next sixty years.

The merger during the war that created the new Norwegian synod was discussed in the previous chapter. In 1918 the General Council, the General Synod and the General Synod South, which had formed during the Civil War, merged to form the United Lutheran Church of America (ULCA). These primarily German bodies, facing the same pressures due to the war, concluded that they needed to put aside their differences and form a more thorough union than any of them had previously been willing to consider. Other Lutheran synods then allied with the ULCA to form a loose confederation. These included the Slovak Zion Synod (which merged into the ULCA in 1920), the Icelandic Synod (which merged into the ULCA in 1942), the Suomi Synod (Finnish), and the American Evangelical Lutheran Church (Danish).

In 1930 the Ohio, Iowa and Buffalo synods merged to form the American Lutheran Church (ALC). The ALC also gathered a group of like-minded churches and formed the American Lutheran Conference. This group was composed of the Norwegian Synod, the Danish Synod, and the Augustana Synod (Swedish). This federation of Lutheran synods was generally regarded as more moderate, falling between the less doctrinally rigorous ULCA and the more doctrinally rigorous Synodical Conference. It tried to balance doctrinal matters against the practical considerations of operating a religious body in twentieth century America.

Neo-Orthodoxy

Neo-orthodoxy[3] had begun before the start of the twentieth century, but did not make much progress until the jolt of World War I. Up until that point Theological Liberalism had been dominant in mainline Protestant circles, particularly in Europe. The war ruined the dreams of the world evolving into a paradise through natural processes. Neo-orthodoxy was born as a means of strengthening Christianity by using, rather than discarding, the terminology of the Bible, but also by removing the requirement that the Bible be understood literally. In some respects, it was a return to the allegorical world of Origen in the second century, where nothing had to mean what it said. Neo-orthodoxy allowed those who wanted to believe the Bible as it was written to do so, but it did not require such a belief to be a good church member. Three men became well-known writers in the movement.

Soren Kierkegaard (1813–55),[4] the first famous contributor, lived long before neo-orthodoxy gained traction. However, he wrote in Danish and was ignored until his books were translated into other languages at the beginning of the twentieth century. Even after being translated, his works were often difficult to understand on account of his extensive use of metaphors, irony, and parables. He differentiated between the biblical proof-text version of Christianity and the individual's subjective relationship with the God-man Jesus Christ. He taught that faith was generated through the emotions and feelings of the individual rather than by the Holy Spirit working through the means of grace. People learned to be subjective in their beliefs.

Karl Barth (1886–1968),[5] a Swiss Reformed theologian, was the most-recognized leader of the movement. He began his theological career with a commentary on Romans. It pointed the reader away from Theological Liberalism toward the importance of knowing God only through Christ. The problem, however, was how to know Christ, and here Barth did not return to the theology of the sixteenth century. Instead he realized, as his theological understanding developed, that man's ability to grasp Christ needed to be greater than just "book faith." He started writing a five-volume work on dogmatics, but he did

---

[3] D. J. Hall, *Remembered Voices: Reclaiming the Legacy of "Neo-Orthodoxy"* (Louisville: Westminster John Knox, 1998).

[4] William Hubben, *Dostoevsky, Kierkegaard, Nietzsche, and Kafka: Four Prophets of Our Destiny* (New York: Collier Books, 1962).

[5] Paul S. Chung, *Karl Barth: God's Word in Action* (Cambridge: James Clarke & Co, 2008).

not quite get through the fourth volume before his death. He became well-known outside the university theological circles, and Pope Pius XII said he was the greatest theologian since Thomas Aquinas. Barth supported the underground church that formed in Germany during the time of the Nazis. One of his associates in the underground church was **Dietrich Bonhoeffer** (1906–45),[6] a young German pastor and professor who had been active in the ecumenical movement before he was executed by the Nazis. Bonhoeffer wrote *The Cost of Discipleship*.

Rudolf Bultmann (1884–1976)[7] was a Lutheran professor of the New Testament at the University of Marburg. He was a prominent critic of Theological Liberalism, who became known for his reliance on demythologizing biblical texts of the New Testament. Bultmann argued that historical analysis of the New Testament was unnecessary. The details of Jesus's life were unimportant; only his existence, his preaching, and his death by crucifixion mattered. He maintained that the Christian faith required the proclamation of the New Testament but not of any particular facts regarding the historical Jesus. Bultmann's rejection of Liberalism was not a return to biblical truth, but merely to the use of terms that made traditional Christians more comfortable.

Changes in Lutheranism after World War II

While the neo-orthodox movement was led by theologians in Europe, it had a major impact on Lutherans in the United States. Most Lutheran synods had participated in the military chaplaincy program during World War I. Lutheran pastors became closely involved with clergymen from other church bodies because the Protestant chaplains often had to serve a diverse mix of Christian believers. After the war this new relationship among members of all Protestant churches led to more exchanges of faculty members and students among Protestant seminaries. It caused the teachings of these church bodies to become more consistent across denominational boundaries. This trend also spilled over into Lutheran seminaries, which began exchanging faculty members and students with each other and sometimes with other Protestant seminaries. Teachers of Neo-orthodox theology became common in the seminaries of the ULCA and then spread into the seminaries of the American Lutheran

---

6   Charles Marsh, *Strange Glory: A Life of Dietrich Bonhoeffer* (New York: Knopf, 2014).
7   Tim Labron, *Bultmann Unlocked* (London: T&T Clark, 2011).

Conference. This situation was further advanced by World War II, in which even more chaplains were involved and even more contacts among the various church bodies occurred.

By the end of the war, a common front on important doctrinal issues was evolving among what has come to be known as "mainline Protestantism," including churches such as the Methodists, the Presbyterians, the Episcopalians, and the American Baptists. The same process was happening within the Lutheran conferences and, to some extent, between the conferences. For example, there were discussions between the Missouri Synod and the ALC about establishing fellowship. Such fellowship would have brought the churches in two of the conferences into closer alignment. A fellowship plan was drafted, but it faced strong opposition from the other members of the Synodical Conference. After several revisions, the plan was dropped in 1960 when the members of the American Lutheran Conference voted to merge into a single synod called The American Lutheran Church (TALC). Also in 1960, church bodies associated with the ULCA voted to merge to form the Lutheran Church in America (LCA). The Augustana Synod switched allegiance to join the LCA.

Another effort to bring Lutheran churches together was the Lutheran World Federation formed in 1947. This group attracted most of the Lutheran bodies from around the world, but not the members of the Synodical Conference. Its doctrinal standard was loose, and it was dominated by churches willing to have religious working relationships with other Protestant groups.

The Ecumenical Movement

The urge to merge was not restricted to Lutherans. Mainline Protestant groups formed a working group called the Consultation on Church Unity (COCU) in 1962, which sought to define the issues dividing the Protestant churches and to find ways to resolve them. Resolution, however, was not always possible when facing doctrinal issues, so organizational solutions were sought. It soon became apparent, however, that the organizational issues were even more difficult to resolve. Too many people were more dedicated to their ways of worship and their organizational structures than they were to the message they preached and the doctrines they held. In the end, organizational considerations were too great to overcome. After years of frustration, in 2002 the members of the COCU scaled back their goals and changed their name to Churches Uniting in Christ.

In the same era, there was an effort to find doctrinal unity through semi-annual meetings of the Jesus Seminar.[8] Several hundred ecumenical theologians from numerous Christian bodies gathered and discussed the statements of Jesus contained in the gospels. They then voted as to whether Jesus had definitely said a particular statement attributed to him, whether he probably said it, whether he might have said something vaguely related to the subject or whether he definitely did not say it. By this democratic folly over a ten-year period, these theologians concluded that Jesus had not said most of what the Bible attributes to him. That this passed for scholarship shows the sorry state of much of Christianity.

The Dissolution of the Synodical Conference

The beginning of the twentieth century saw continued growth in the Synodical Conference with the Nebraska Synod and the Slovak Synod joining in 1908. The Nebraska Synod merged into the Wisconsin Synod in 1917, following the consolidation plan previous proposed (see chapter 12). The Norwegian Synod of the American Evangelical Lutheran Church joined the Conference in 1920. After this, there were no further changes until the 1950s. However, each of the member church bodies changed its name, creating initials that became part of the Lutheran alphabet soup. The Missouri Synod became the Lutheran Church-Missouri Synod (LCMS). The Wisconsin Synod became the Wisconsin Evangelical Lutheran Synod (WELS). The Norwegian Synod of the American Evangelical Lutheran Church became the Evangelical Lutheran Synod (ELS). The Slovak Synod became the Synod of Evangelical Lutheran Churches (SELC).

Differences over the doctrine of church fellowship came to a head in the 1940s among the synods of the Synodical Conference. These gained important when the LCMS began exploratory talks about fellowship with the ALC, as previously mentioned. Because the ALC's position on the doctrine of election was the same as that of the old Ohio Synod, the other members of the Synodical Conference became suspicious of the actions of the LCMS. After prolonged discussions within the Conference, the ELS severed fellowship with the LCMS in 1955, and the WELS severed fellowship with the LCMS in 1961. In the meantime, 70 pastors and congregations, feeling that the

---

[8] Robert W. Funk, *The Gospel of Jesus: According to the Jesus Seminar*, 2nd ed. (Salem Oregon: Polebridge Press, 2015).

WELS had not acted quickly enough, left it to form the Church of the Lutheran Confession (CLC) in 1955. The Conference dissolved in 1963.

The dissolution of the Synodical Conference focused on the issue of fellowship, and this issue involved various matters dating back to World War I. Other Conference members had objected to the LCMS's participation in the military chaplaincy program and its relationship with the Boy Scouts. The talks between the LCMS and the ALC intensified the concern over its doctrine of church fellowship. In addition, there was the well-founded suspicion that neo-orthodoxy was creeping into the LCMS seminary in St. Louis.

Difficulties Within the LCMS

The troubles for the LCMS were only beginning, however. It joined the Lutheran Council in the USA (LCUSA) with TALC and the LCA in the middle 1960s. In 1969 the LCMS selected Dr. John Tietjen, a proponent of neo-orthodoxy, to be president of its St. Louis seminary. This caused outrage throughout many parts of the LCMS. It resulted in Dr. Jacob Preus being elected LCMS president, replacing Oliver Harms. Preus ordered a study to be made of the theology of the St. Louis faculty members based on their public statements, conference presentations and personal interviews. This led to a struggle over doctrinal matters at the seminary which lasted for several years and led to the suspension of Tietjen in 1974. Most of the faculty members and students walked out in support of him. The board of control removed the faculty members who walked out and suspended the students. The departing group formed a seminary-in-exile known as Seminex. It and its supporters barnstormed the LCMS, trying to get its graduates accepted into the ministry. At first, it appeared they had a lot of support from district presidents and congregations, but much of the support disappeared when it became necessary to actually accept the graduates. After an LCMS national convention condemned Seminex and its supporters, they withdrew and formed the Association of Evangelical Lutheran Churches (AELC).

The LCMS began to retreat from the pan-Lutheran movement after the departure of the AELC members. In 1977 it withdrew from the LCUSA. In 1981 it withdrew from its fellowship agreement with TALC into which it had hesitantly entered in 1969. Internally, the struggles left the LCMS in disarray, but it had not become sucked into the merger mania of the LCUSA. In 1988 the AELC, TALC and the LCA merged to form the Evangelical Lutheran Church in America (ELCA). This spawned numerous splinter groups that objected to the lack of doctrinal unity. The ELCA accepted the Lutheran Confessions only in their historical setting and not as binding in all matters of doctrine which they cover. The ELCA has been calving groups of disgruntled pastors and congregations since its formation. Lutherans who believed in the verbal inspiration of the Scriptures and insisted on accepting the Lutheran Confessions as a standard of faith, albeit as a secondary standard to the Scriptures, began more formally calling themselves "Confessional Lutherans" in the late 1980s.[9] This group included the LCMS, the WELS, the ELS, the CLC and perhaps a few other synods in the changing Lutheran landscape.

Secular Humanism

In the 1850s, Englishmen George Holyoake and Charles Bradlaugh started a movement they called "secularism." It has since become known as "Secular Humanism" or Humanism with a capital "H." Its goal was to establish a moral code independent of any religion, a code which could be tested by scientific evidence and human experience. Within a generation, societies began forming in major American cities which supported the concept of morality without religion. Humanists emphasized that 1) Morality changes as civilization advances; 2) Philanthropy is a moral obligation in advanced societies; 3) Self-reform is as necessary as social reform; 4) Governments must become democratic; and 5) Education is of central importance.

Secular Humanism was the driving force behind the rise of the intelligentsia in Russia in the late nineteenth century in opposition to the Tsarist government. It was the seedbed for socialist movements across Europe before World War I. In Russia militant Humanists formed the Communist Party which, under the leadership of Vladimir Lenin, toppled the provisional government that had ousted the Tsar. After World War I, Humanists split into two camps. One favored democratic socialism, and the other favored soviet communism. Reaction to the growing power of the Humanists in Europe came from groups known as fascists. These opposed the philosophy of universal democracy. Economic conditions strengthened the fascists, who, like the Humanists, worshiped the glories of human achievements. Fascists captured Italy, Spain and

---

[9] The name "Confessional Lutheran" had been used informally before, but the need to emphasize a separation from Lutherans who only accepted the Lutheran Confessions as historical documents became essential during this era.

Germany for their cause. In Germany, racism combined with fascism to produce the dreaded Nazis and another world war.

World War II had two opposite effects on the Humanist movement, particularly in the United States. War, famine, and plagues made more people seek
God, and this was very evident in the American culture of the 1950s and the
early 1960s. Conversely, the war brought Humanists together as well. Expanded college faculties were needed to handle the influx of soldiers seeking
a higher education. This allowed the entry of numerous Humanists into the
new teaching positions and placed a captive audience before them, permitting
them to train the next generation of activists. Although the "Red Scare"[10]
slowed the growth of their efforts temporarily, the anti-colonial and civil
rights movements around the world reinvigorated the forces of Humanism.

Mohandas Gandhi (1869–1948),[11] an Indian lawyer, was the prototype for
civil rights leaders of the twentieth century. Gandhi was born into a Hindu
family. He began his civil rights campaigning in South Africa, where he developed the principles of non-violent civil disobedience. He lived there for 21
years before he returned to India in 1915. He immediately began organizing
farmers, peasants, and urban workers against land taxes and discrimination.
As head of the Indian National Congress, he campaigned against poverty, the
subjugation of women, and colonialism and for numerous Humanist goals.
He adopted the traditional clothing of the Indian poor. His civil disobedience
often led to his arrest and imprisonment. While his work greatly advanced the
cause of independence for India in 1947, much to his dismay, colonial India
was split into two (now three) countries due to the hostility between Hindus
and Muslims. Gandhi was assassinated by a Hindu nationalist.

Martin Luther King, Jr. (1929–68),[12] although nominally an American Baptist minister, was a devoted disciple of Gandhi. Beginning in Birmingham,
Alabama, he gained prominence because of his "non-violent" actions and

---

[10] The "Red Scare" was a national hysteria in the United States in the late 1940s and early
1950s caused by the fear that Communists were infiltrating the infrastructure of America
and selling its secrets to the Soviet Union.

[11] Anne M. Todd, *Mohandas Gandhi* (New York: Infobase Publishing, 2009).

"Mahatma" was a title of respect by which Gandhi was known and not his first name.

[12] Marshall Frady, *Martin Luther King, Jr.: A Life* (New York: Penguin, 2002).

He was named Michael King, Jr. at birth, but his father, who was a pastor, later changed
his own name and that of his son to strengthen the appeal of his ministry.

rhetoric, as well as his speaking ability. The television networks favored him over other civil rights leaders who advocated more confrontational or violent courses to prevent triggering a race war. The lopsided Democratic election victory in 1964 and numerous court decisions led to massive changes in the national laws. These changes gave Black Americans a chance for equality after a century of discrimination following their emancipation from slavery.

Civil rights changes, however, went far beyond establishing racial equality. They were used to inject the principles of Secular Humanism into every aspect of American life, dethroning Christianity as the *de facto* religion in America. Secular Humanism and its civil rights sect must indeed be classified as religious movements based on the dedicated behavior of their adherents and their proclamation of a new morality. Lutherans were slow to recognize the face of a new type of false religion. In recent years, the ELCA has seen numerous congregations withdraw from it over its adoption of Humanistic principles in place of biblical teachings.

Postmodernism

Perhaps the most perplexing idea to develop in the twentieth century has been called "Postmodernism." Since the time of Isaac Newton, intellectuals have considered the secular world to be in a period which they have referred to as "modernity." It has been a period of rational thought, reliable rules of nature, and a middle-class morality that emerged from an uneasy alliance between classical humanism and Christianity. The advance of Secular Humanism in Western Society changed people's willingness to be bound by any laws formulated by others, whether through religious teachings or through popular consensus. According to this philosophy, each person has his or her own standard of right and wrong. Proofs mean nothing. There are no absolutes. Gender, for example, comes in many varieties, not just two.

These ideas can be traced back to Descartes and German philosopher **Georg Hegel** (1770–1831).[13] These concepts did not become popular earlier because no society had been rich enough to embrace such ideas before the latter part of the twentieth century.[14] In the first part of the twenty-first century, these ideas have become part of the American body politic, primarily as a

---

[13] Howard P. Kainz, *G. W. F. Hegel* (Athens, Ohio: Ohio University Press, 1996).
[14] When people are struggling to reach a basic level of prosperity in terms of material goods, they have little interest in such abstract philosophy.

result of court decisions. This situation harks back to the time of the judges in Israel, when there was no central authority and when everyone did what was right in his own eyes.[15] Under the influence of this philosophy, more and more people are becoming atheists and agnostics. It will hasten the decline of Christianity in America, at least until some new global crisis occurs.

Twentieth Century Lutheranism in Germany

The end of World War I left the Protestant churches in Germany in disarray. An effort to unify German Protestantism occurred during the Weimar Republic, creating a confederation which existed from 1922 until 1933. Adolf Hitler tried to reorganize this confederation into a united pro-Nazi Protestant church. This effort totally failed, and the confederation fragmented. Hitler arrested numerous pastors who opposed his *Reichskirche*.

The Evangelical Church in Germany (EKD) is the latest reincarnation of the remnants of the Prussian Union. It is a federation of twenty nominally Lutheran, Reformed and United regional churches. It was originally formed in 1948, ruptured in 1969, and reunited in 1991 after the fall of the Berlin Wall. Its membership is less than half that of the Church of the Prussian Union before World War I. All its member churches share pulpit and altar fellowship though they hold different teachings on many issues.

Confessional Lutheranism in America

Now, early in the twenty-first century, things are not looking favorable for Confessional Lutheranism. There are fewer people today who can be classified as Confessional Lutherans than there were at the beginning of the twentieth century. Membership in Confessional Lutheran synods continues to decline. There are numerous factors that can be cited, but as always, the primary cause is the underuse of the Word of God. This is coupled with a general cowardliness in spreading the Word in a society which has grown more hostile to it. We will look at the dangers threatening Confessional Lutheranism in the next chapter. They are indeed daunting, because as Pogo,[16] a cartoon character from long ago, once said, "We have met the enemy, and he is us."

---

[15] "In those days there was no king in Israel, and every man did whatever was right in his own eyes." (Judges 17:6)
[16] Pogo was the central character in a syndicated cartoon strip of the same name by Walter Kelly, Jr.

14

Walking in Danger
AD 2020–Judgment Day

History did not end with yesterday. Each day its journal grows longer. Someday our actions, both the praiseworthy and the regrettable, will be written in that journal of history for others to read. In this last chapter we will look at some areas of our actions as Confessional Lutherans that may draw condemnation from future generations if we do not handle them well.

Few things are more difficult than honestly evaluating oneself. We are all blind by nature to our own errors and tend to dismiss them as trivial when others call them to our attention. To the members of each generation, it seems impossible that they will be the generation that allows the pure message of God's Word to become polluted or slip away because they see themselves as so committed to it. Any open-minded reader of the previous chapters should be convinced of how foolish such self-confidence is. St. Paul wrote, "So let him who thinks he stands be careful that he does not fall."[1] Every faithful church organization is in Satan's gunsights. He is going to continually pressure it in countless ways to weaken and destroy it. If we do not see this happening, then we should become alarmed because it means Satan has already succeeded. History tells us that every organization of God's people will be led astray unless it periodically purges accumulated dross. Let us prepare ourselves by doing a brief review of the history of religious backsliding.

Moses warned the Israelites, "When you eat and are satisfied, and you build nice houses and move into them, and your herds and your flocks multi-

---

[1]   1 Corinthians 10:12.

ply, and your silver and gold increase, and everything that you have prospers, watch out so that your heart does not become arrogant and forget the LORD your God, who brought you out of the land of Egypt, where you were slaves."[2] When things are going well, people are always tempted to believe that they have everything under control and, as a result, congratulate themselves on their own acumen. So it was with Israel. During the period of the judges, the Israelites fell away from the LORD repeatedly. The LORD rescued them, but once the God-sent deliverer had died, they quickly went back to idols. Under the kings of the unified kingdom and of Judah, it was the same story. After they had been put on the right path by a good king and/or a good high priest, within a generation or two they were deep into paganism. Even the "good" kings overlooked the idolatry being practiced outside Jerusalem, paving the way for the next relapse.

Since the coming of Christ, things have been no better. Paul's ministry was troubled by false teachers. In the letters to the seven churches in Revelation, Jesus came down hard on straying congregations.[3] The early centuries of the church were plagued with heresy after heresy. The Roman Catholic Church spiraled downward as false doctrine mounted during the Middle Ages. After Luther's death, the Philippists troubled the Lutheran church. They were followed by Pietism, Rationalism, Theological Liberalism, and Neo-orthodoxy. The Ohio Synod lost its bearings over the doctrine of election and fell away from confessionalism over time. The Wisconsin Synod was troubled by the Protes'tant Controversy,[4] and the Missouri Synod nearly landed in the theological dumpster at the time of the Seminex incident. Not only can we lose the pure gospel, but history strongly suggests that we will, just like so many others. Fear of being dragged from the narrow Lutheran middle path should cause every true Confessional Lutheran—pastor and layperson—to continually return to God's Word and to beg the LORD that he preserve his pure doctrine among us. We should not be looking at ourselves and rejoicing at how well we have kept the faith. The LORD does not let us see the future, but the pattern of the past should be enough to get our attention.

---

[2]   Deuteronomy 8:12–14.

[3]   Jesus said, "I know your works, that you are neither cold nor hot. If only you were cold or hot! So, because you are lukewarm and not hot or cold, I am about to spit you out of my mouth." (Revelation 3:15, 16).

[4]   The Protes'tant Controversy arose in the Wisconsin Synod following the presentation of a theological paper by Pastor W. F. Beitz in 1926. This dispute led to a number of people with different grievances uniting and leaving the synod.

In this chapter we will consider some of the dangers that are threatening Confessional Lutheranism in America. We will look at them in terms of the twofold mission of the church, namely, to train its members and to evangelize the unbelievers. Our marching orders are the Great Commandment[5] and the Great Commission.[6] We must look at our actions from God's perspective and not our own. We must consider whether we are alert to the real dangers. We must examine whether we have become dedicated to the means rather than the message. These are common problems in organizations, and if they are not fixed, they become fatal. We must examine both our deeds and our hearts. The LORD will forgive us, and the Holy Spirit will aid us, but not if we cover our eyes and plug our ears.

The Danger of the Shrunken God

The people of the world do not want to recognize the God of the Bible. This is natural because they are servants of Satan. In our era they react to the biblical God by trying to shrink him. They place restrictions on what he can do. They resculpt him to remove from him those attributes that trouble them. They squeeze him into a closet until they need him. They make him generic so that he fits with every religion. As Confessional Lutherans we are exposed to this revisionist God every day, and the constant misrepresentation will wear away our knowledge of the LORD if we do not constantly review the nature of our God. If our God becomes distorted by our changing his attributes, then we are believing in a worthless idol.

Our faith in God must come from the Word of God. Moses began the Great Commandment by reminding the Israelites who their God was. People cannot believe in a God about whom they know little.[7] The members of our congregations must know the details about the LORD that the Bible reveals to us. This

---

5   [Moses said,] "Hear, O Israel! The LORD is our God. The LORD is one! Love the LORD your God with all your heart and with all your soul and with all your might. These words that I am commanding you today are to be on your heart. Teach them diligently to your children, and speak about them when you sit in your house and when you walk on the road, when you lie down and when you get up. Tie them as a sign on your wrists, and they will serve as symbols on your forehead. Write them on the doorposts of your houses and on your gates." (Deuteronomy 6:4–9)

6   [Jesus said,] "All authority in heaven and on earth has been given to me. Therefore go and gather disciples from all nations by baptizing them in the name of the Father and of the Son and of the Holy Spirit, and by teaching them to keep all the instructions I have given you." (Matthew 28:18–20)

7   "How can they believe in the one about whom they have not heard?" (Romans 10:14)

requires that the attributes of God must be regularly presented in sermons and in Bible classes. The laity must be directed to regularly study the attributes of God in their expanded catechisms. Without this emphasis, many of our lay-people will be worshipers of a generic god. It has happened to others; it will happen to us if we don't commit ourselves to assiduously knowing the LORD.

The Danger of Half-Hearted Commitment

The people who with some regularity show up for worship services are committed Christians. So are the shut-ins who are always eager to see the pastor. But are they committed to Christ or only to the society of the local congregation? Would it matter to them what was being preached provided the format of worship and the structure of the organization remained the same? How much of their lives are invested in their religion?

Once people know who the LORD is, they need to understand what commitment to the LORD really means. The Israelites were reminded of their commitment to their God by the ceremonial laws that regulated many activities in their daily lives. In the New Testament times we have not been given a list of specific actions to perform and specific unclean things to avoid. Yet God expects to be imbedded in our daily lives. How that is accomplished is an adiaphoron; that it must be accomplished is not! Placing God first in our lives cannot be an idle statement or a "stretch goal." The LORD must be a living presence in the life of each member of our congregations, and each member needs to have a plan, periodically evaluated and updated, to accomplish this. The Great Commandment is not merely a divine suggestion.

The last four verses of the Great Commandment tell about the type of activities that those who take the commandment seriously engage in. They spend their time in the Word. It permeates the activities of their lives. It is a constant presence. Psalm 1:2 says of the believer, "His delight is in the teaching of the LORD, and on his teaching he meditates day and night." The Christian life is a life of commitment to the study of God's Word. It is not a life of mere passive acceptance of facts. If there is not a driving desire to know the LORD better, then there is no saving faith. To the church in Sardis Jesus said, "I know your works. You have a reputation for being alive, but you are dead."[8] To the church in Laodicea he said, "Because you are lukewarm and not hot or

---

[8]   Revelation 3:1.

cold, I am about to spit you out of my mouth."[9] The urgency of getting church members to understand this matter cannot be overstated.

The Danger of Losing the Lutheran Heritage

By the strength and with the guidance of the LORD, Martin Luther and his colleagues gave us a treasure of unfathomable worth which had been lost for centuries due to the unfaithfulness of previous church leaders. As seen in the preceding chapters, the struggles to keep this treasure once it had been regained were arduous because Satan was determined to snuff out the light of the gospel. Yet as Lutherans today we cannot rest on the work of our spiritual fathers, thinking the battle has been won. Daily the hosts of hell are trying to undermine the biblical teachings of our Confessional Lutheran churches.

Sadly, to the world, and often to ourselves, Confessional Lutherans are just another Protestant group. Why is this true? Because Lutheran congregations are not emphasizing their Lutheran heritage and what it means. Luther stood before the Diet of Worms on April 18, 1521, and refused to recant. How many Lutheran congregations celebrate this day? June 25, 1530, was the date on which Dr. Christian Beyer read the Augsburg Confession to Charles V. How many Lutheran congregations celebrate this date, the birthday of the Lutheran church? How many lay Lutherans own a copy of the Lutheran Confessions and have read them? Our forefathers' labors are being lost through our indifference. As we forget these men and their struggles, we will also lessen the value of the teachings which they worked so hard to keep pure.

Martin Luther did not die to save us, and his writings were not given by verbal inspiration. On the other hand, Luther and his sixteenth century colleagues gave us an approach to the study of God's Word which allows the Holy Spirit to use it to preserve the faith of the saints. If we want to call ourselves Confessional Lutherans, then we must value and preserve the treasure they have given us. If we do not, then unlike Luther, we will have recanted what we promised on the day of our confirmation. It is imperative that every Lutheran pastor lead his sheep to crave the pure Word of God and that the sheep urge their pastors to train them more thoroughly in the Word.[10]

---

[9] Revelation 3:16.
[10] "Therefore rid yourselves of all evil, all deceit, hypocrisy, jealousy, and all slander. Like newborn babies, crave the pure milk of the word so that by it you may grow up with the result being salvation." (1 Peter 2:1, 2)

The Danger of Arminian Infiltration

We live in a world where Christianity is dominated by Arminianism. Aspects of Arminian theology are influential in many mainline Protestant church bodies and in much of American Evangelicalism. It has even penetrated the Roman Catholic and Lutheran churches. It is prominent on Christian talk radio and in the books available through Zondervan. While there are many features of Arminian theology that are troubling, the one that creates the greatest danger is its emphasis on the individual's role in coming to and remaining in the faith. Let us call this "I" theology. It is shown clearly in the sequence: "The Bible says it. I believe it. That settles it." The sentence "I believe it" is irrelevant to the truth of the Bible. When we put it in this position, we give our reason a role in establishing spiritual truth. While Evangelicals, depending on their flavor, may strongly defend biblical truths, somewhere in their affirmation will appear something that indicates they believe they have an active role in the saving process. Their part may seem small, but it is synergistic nonetheless. Their "I" theology appears in many of the books and hymns they write.

In contrast, Lutherans believe in a theology in which we are always the object of, not an actor in, the events that save us. We have nothing to contribute to our redemption, to our conversion, or to the preservation of our faith. That is what *sola gratia* is all about. It is not just that God has done great things for me; it is that he has done *everything* for me. In Lutheran theology, the phrases "I know," "I believe" and "I act" can solely be said based on the faith that the Holy Spirit has worked in me. I must take no credit.[11] To prevent being led astray, all Lutherans need to understand this difference.

Arminian theology is seductive because it makes people feel good about being Christians. People feel a sense of accomplishment, which can be enhanced by self-improvement schemes. Arminianism teaches that in improving oneself, one becomes more worthy of God's grace and can therefore be more certain of one's own salvation. The longer and harder one works, the more secure one feels.[12] Again, the "I" theology comes to the forefront. This is the exact opposite of Lutheranism. The longer people are Lutherans, the

---

[11] The famous "Here I stand" statement attributed to Luther at the Diet of Worms must be understood in its context. It is not in the official transcript, and if it was said, it was probably said in German. The key words in his statement were, "My conscience is captive to the Word of God." His stance was not about what he was doing but about the Word of God.

[12] This is sometimes referred to as the "theology of glory."

more they learn of God's Law, of their own unworthiness, and of their need for a Savior. "God, be merciful to *me*, a sinner!"[13] It is natural for people to be tempted to smuggle a little Arminian theology into the Lutheran church to add an increased sense of personal satisfaction to their faith. It is imperative that we test every idea (i.e., every spirit) to see that it really is faithful to God's Word and has a place in the Lutheran church.[14] This includes the hymns we use in our churches and the books we use in our schools. We need to assume nothing is harmless,[15] even if it comes from other "Christian" sources, until it is tested.[16]

The Danger of the Loss of Missionary Zeal

The Great Commission must be the driver of the actions of the church. The members of the early church were few in a society of many, but they understood the Commission's importance and were willing to die to carry it out. Then, for many centuries almost everyone in much of Europe was nominally Christian. The responsibility for telling people about Jesus passed from the individual Christians to the church organizational. The clergy liked it that way and did not want the laity to know and spread the teachings of the Bible. Luther reintroduced the responsibility for teaching the Christian message within the family, but there was little need for people to reach outside the family in communities where nearly everyone was already Lutheran. The zeal to spread the message was not stoked. Even when Lutherans found themselves in communities with numerous unchurched people, as they did in America, they followed their deeply ingrained custom of speaking about their religious beliefs only with their fellow Lutherans.

In American society religion is an easy subject to avoid. We do not want anyone to become angry with us. We tell ourselves that we have our own lives to live and that maybe our neighbors will start going to church if they see us going. Perhaps a few will, but even getting people to sit in our churches is not

---

[13] Prayer of the tax collector in Luke 18:13.

[14] "Dear friends, do not believe every spirit, but test the spirits to see if they are from God, for many false prophets have gone out into the world." (1 John 4:1)

[15] "Do you not know that a little yeast leavens the whole batch of dough?" (1 Corinthians 5:6)

[16] Reliance on the magisterial use of human reason is an inherent characteristic of American Evangelical theology. A sad example of this is its infatuation with creation science. This topic is not within the scope of this book. Readers should consult *Clearing a Path for the Gospel – A Lutheran Approach to Apologetics* by Arthur A. Eggert and Geoffrey A. Kieta (Sun Prairie, Wisconsin: In Terra Pax Lutheran Publishing, 2019).

the ultimate goal of mission work. We need to reach people's minds with the saving message so the Holy Spirit can change their hearts. That takes a lot more effort than just getting someone to come into our church building. If they want to join our congregation and remain an active part of it, they will need help in understanding the teachings of the Scriptures long after the pastor finishes his basic doctrine course. Our members need to prepare themselves to help other members, particularly newer members, grow in their faith and their understanding of God's Word. The Savior is calling all of us to work in his spiritual vineyard, not just in the church organizational.

The reason most Confessional Lutherans are such bad evangelists is that they are not bursting to tell others about Jesus Christ; they are dreading that they might have to. Those who do not engage in the lifelong practice of applying the mirror of the law and the grace of God to themselves will not have the joy of salvation that they want others to know, a joy which comes from active repentance. Because most Lutherans do not study the biblical teachings so that they know what they need to say, they are afraid someone might ask questions that they cannot answer. Therefore, they clam up. Church outreach, in which we merely show our congregation's flag in the community, rather than evangelism, where we actually talk to people about our LORD, has come to predominate, if anything is being done at all. First, Lutherans need to learn more; then Lutherans need to tell more. We should not fear that we are alone; the LORD is with us.[17] We cannot wait for a more opportune time. There is a spiritual war on, and we have been called to duty.

The Danger in Theocracy

The Israelites is the Old Testament lived in a theocracy. They were God's chosen people living in a nation governed by God's civil laws. As members of the Christian church today, we are also God's chosen people, but we do not live in a theocracy. That "In God we trust" appears on our money and that "one nation under God" is included in the Pledge of Alliance do not mean that America is the LORD's special nation or that it should be governed by God's Old Testament laws. In fact, the "god" mentioned in the phrases above is only a generic god, not the Lord God of the Bible. Today, there is nothing special

---

[17]   [Jesus said,] "Surely I am with you always until the end of the age." (Matthew 28:20)

about any nation in God's eyes, and he has ordained no link between our churches and the government at any level.

There is nothing inherently wrong about being patriotic. Jeremiah tells the Jews in Babylon to pray and work for the good of the nation of their captors.[18] Paul urges Christians to be law-abiding citizens of their nations.[19] Lutherans are also citizens of cities, states, provinces, and countries to which they have legal obligations. Although the church can cooperate with the state on activities of mutual interest, the church must not use its moral authority to promote the programs of the state. The symbols and heroes of the state are not the symbols and heroes of the church. These should not be confused or mixed. Nations come and nations go, but the kingdom of the LORD abides forever. The church exists solely to promote the latter kingdom. Its pulpits must not be used to foster the political agendas of the preachers.

Dangers in the Church Organizational

As the years have passed, many in Confessional Lutheranism have come to equate good organization with faithfulness to the mission of the church. If one's congregation has programs and/or committees to address all the issues, Lutherans have come to think that matters are in hand, and there is nothing to worry about. God, after all, will bless the well-organized. Yet, a well-polished organization can easily conceal a church which is little more than a social association of pleasant people with enough trappings of religion to make the parishioners feel pious. We will look briefly at several areas of concern whose detailed discussion is beyond the scope of this book.

Religious Materialism: "I deserve" has become the motto of America's consumer society, and we are all tempted to buy into the excess. Yet, the things of heavenly wealth are not compatible with the things of earthly wealth, which is why it is so hard for rich people, like most of us, to enter heaven. The physical things people own are often idols that own their owners' souls. Certainly, preaching needs to be strong and specific on this matter, but laypeople also need to enumerate God's blessings rather than to enlarge their wish lists.

---

18 "Seek the peace of the city where I have exiled you. Pray to the LORD for that city, because when it has peace and prosperity, you will have peace and prosperity." (Jeremiah 29:7)

19 "Remind them to be subject to rulers and authorities, to obey, to be ready to do any good work, to speak evil of no one, to be peaceable, to be gentle, and to display every courtesy toward all people." (Titus 3:1–2)

Moreover, personal greed has spread to people's church life so that materialism exists in many Lutheran congregations and schools. A church may be spending little or no money and effort on evangelism and elders' work, but it strives to have an ideal place of worship or an impressive sports facility. To brag about one's facilities is always a temptation. Yet, we must ask, "How many of those who worshiped in the beautiful Catholic cathedrals of Europe were saved? The LORD is only impressed by the quality of our faith, not the magnificence of our buildings and programs. It is easy to condemn the Israelites for forsaking the LORD in their prosperity, but do we have our eyes more on the methods and mechanisms than the mission of spreading the message?

Worship Format: In the Old Testament the LORD prescribed in great detail the manner in which the Israelites were to worship him. Yet, even at those times in their history when they followed the prescribed liturgies and animal sacrifices, the LORD was often unhappy with them.[20] In the New Testament the format of worship is not prescribed; it is an adiaphoron. This point should not be forgotten by pastors when they are preparing worship services. The purpose of worship is helping the congregation members grow in their faith, in their understanding of God's Word, and in their trust in their LORD. The laity must understand that just attending church and going through the liturgy, no matter how beautiful, does not aid in their salvation *ex opere operato*.

Christian Education: Solomon wrote, "Dedicate a child to the way he should go, and even when he becomes old, he will not turn away from it."[21] Children need to be brought to understand that their commitment to the service of the LORD must be the first thing in their lives from the time they can understand anything. That commitment must underlie all their choices in life—their profession, their spouse, the location of their residence, and even their hobbies. The salvation of their souls is at stake.

The traditional Lutheran elementary school has been the right tool in the past in many places for thoroughly indoctrinating children in the Lutheran faith and for building a relationship between the school and the parents for proper learning. These goals must always be our top priority. However,

---

[20] "The LORD says: 'These people approach me with their words, and they honor me with their lips, but their hearts are far from me. Their worship of me is nothing but commandments taught by men.' " (Isaiah 29:13)

[21] Proverbs 22:6.

changes in demographics, technology and educational demands have created a need to reevaluate how to accomplish these goals. Children in smaller congregations which cannot afford schools have the same challenges as those in larger churches, and their parents need help in raising them in the faith. We need to consider how to address this. Another important issue is that the teaching materials used in our schools often come from publishers who do not have a Lutheran agenda. This can lead children astray. Pressures on our schools to add additional programs and objectives may compromise our primary goals. We must weigh everything, so we do not lose more than we gain. Our schools need to continually be reassessed in terms of what we need now and will need in the future, without undue reliance on what worked in the past. The message does not change, but the methods do.

Conclusion

This chapter has by no means enumerated all the dangers that the Lutheran church faces. Many of the dangers mentioned must be considered in much greater detail than is consistent with the purpose of a book on church history. What has been mentioned is only to open the door to our examining our work in the LORD's kingdom in the light of the Great Commandment and the Great Commission that we have received.

As Confessional Lutherans we do not have the slightest reason to boast that we have remained faithful believers while the rest of the Christian church has abandoned some or all of the teachings of the Bible. We are what we are completely by God's grace. St. Paul's warning to beware of falling away needs to be continually ringing in our ears. An honest verdict on Confessional Lutheranism is that it is slowly dying through the loss of members and the loss of zeal. It will not solve the former if it does not first solve the latter.

We do need to review what we are doing, but we should not despair. We have the LORD's commission, and we have his promise. Let us renew our confirmation vows to be faithful unto death, study God's Word with all diligence, adhere to all its teachings with tenacity, and proclaim it in every place we can, in season and out of season. It is the LORD's mission, and we have been given the wonderful opportunity of being allowed to be part of it.

Let us give all glory to the LORD for all that he has given to us and let us resolve to tell the world about his salvation.

References and Readings

Aland, Kurt. *A History of Christianity*, Vol. 1. Translated by James L. Schaaf. Philadelphia: Fortress Press, 1985.

Andrae, Tor. *Mohammed: The Man and His Faith*. Translated by Theophil Manzel. Mineola, New York: Dover Publications, 2000.

Baepler, Walther A. *A Century of Grace: A History of the Missouri Synod, 1847–1947*. Saint Louis: Concordia Publishing House, 1947.

Bainton, Roland H. *Here I Stand*. New York: Abingdon Press, 1950.

Barnes, Timothy. *Constantine: Dynasty, Religion and Power in the Later Roman Empire*. Oxford: Blackwell Publishing, 2011.

Benecke, Gerhard. *Germany in the Thirty Years War*. London: St. Martin's Press, 1978.

Benedict XVI, Pope. *Church Fathers: From Clement of Rome to Augustine*. Vatican City: Libreria Editrice Vaticana, 2007.

Bente, F. *Historical Introduction to the Book of Concord*. Saint Louis: Concordia Publishing House, 1965.

Bigler, Robert M. *The Politics of German Protestantism: The Rise of the Protestant Church Elite in Prussia, 1815–1848*. Berkeley: University of California Press, 1972.

Boccaccio, Giovanni. *The Decameron*. Translated by G. H. McWilliam. Franklin Center, Pennsylvania: The Franklin Library, 1981.

Boettcher+Trinklein Television, Inc. *A Return to Grace – Luther's Life and Legacy*. 2017, (Movie).

Bonner, Gerald. *St. Augustine of Hippo: Life and Controversies*. Philadelphia: The Westminster Press, 1963.

Bouwsma, William James. *John Calvin: A Sixteenth-Century Portrait*. New York: Oxford University Press, 1988.

Bowle, John. *Henry VIII: A Study of Power in Action*. Boston: Little, Brown and Company, 1964.

Brandt, Kaspar. *The Life of James Arminius*. London: Ward and Company, 1854.

Brenner, John M. *The Election Controversy Among Lutheran in the Twentieth Century: An Examination of the Underlying Problems*. Milwaukee: epublications.marguette.edu/ dissertations_mu/204).

Broad, C. D. *Kant: An Introduction*. Cambridge: Cambridge University Press, 1978.

Bullock, Karen O. *The Writing of Justin Martyr*. Nashville: Broadman & Holman Publishers, 1998.

Burke, Peter. *The Italian Renaissance: Culture and Society in Italy*. Princeton: Princeton University Press, 1999.

Chemnitz, Martin. *Examination of the Council of Trent*, Vols 1–4. Translated by Fred Kramer. Saint Louis: Concordia Publishing House, 1971.

Chung, Paul S. *Karl Barth: God's Word in Action*. Cambridge: James Clarke & Co, 2008.

Clarke, Desmond. *Descartes: A Biography*. Cambridge: Cambridge University Press, 2006.

Colish, Marcia L. *Peter Lombard*, Vols 1 & 2. New York: E. J. Brill, 1994.

Crouter, Richard. *Friedrich Schleiermacher: Between Enlightenment and Romanticism*. Cambridge: Cambridge University Press: 2008.

Cowdrey, H. E. J. *Pope Gregory VII, 1073–1085*. Oxford: Clarendon Press, 1998.

Dakdok, Usama K. *The Generous Qur'an*. Venice, Florida: Usama Dakdok Publishing, LLC, 2009.

Danby, Herbert, trans. *The Mishnah*. Peabody, Massachusetts: Hendrickson Publishers, 201).

Desmond, Adrian and James Morre. *Darwin*. London: Michael Joseph, Penguin Group, 1991.

Deutschlander, Daniel M. *The Narrow Lutheran Middle*. Milwaukee: Northwestern Publishing House, 2011.

Dudden, H. Homes. *The Life and Times of Gregory I, the Great*. Amazon for Kindle.

———. *The Life and Times of St. Ambrose*. Oxford: Clarendon Press, 1935.

Eggert, Arthur A. *Simply Lutheran*. Milwaukee: Northwestern Publishing House, 2020.

——— and Kieta, Geoffrey A. *Clearing a Path for the Gospel – A Lutheran Approach to Apologetics*. Sun Prairie, Wisconsin: In Terra Pax Lutheran Publishing, 2019.

Emerton, Ephraim. *Desiderius Erasmus of Rotterdam*. New York: G.P. Putnam's Sons, 189).

Engelbrecht, Edward A., ed. *Church History: The Basics*. St. Louis: Concordia Publishing House, 2016.

Ferguson, Everett, ed. *Encyclopedia of Early Christianity*. New York: Garland Publishing, 1997.

Fortin, John, ed. *Saint Anselm: His Origins and Influence*. Lewiston, New York: Edwin Mellen Press, 2001.

Frady, Marshall. *Martin Luther King, Jr.: A Life*. New York: Penguin, 2002.

Funk, Robert W. *The Gospel of Jesus: According to the Jesus Seminar*, 2nd ed. Salem Oregon: Polebridge Press, 2015.

Glahe, F. *Adam Smith and the Wealth of Nations: 1776–1976*. Boulder, Colorado: University Press of Colorado, 1977.

Gottlieb, Anthony. *The Dream of Enlightenment: The Rise of Modern Philosophy*. London: W. W. Norton & Company, 2016.

Grob, Jean. *The Life of Ulric Zwingli*. New York: Funk & Wagnalls, 1883.

Hall, D. J. *Remembered Voices: Reclaiming the Legacy of "Neo-Orthodoxy"*. Louisville: Westminster John Knox, 1998.

Harrison, Alan. *John Toland (1670–1722)*. Baile Átha Cliath: Coiscéim, 1994.

Healy, Nicholas M. *Thomas Aquinas: Theologian of the Christian Life*. Farnham, UK: Ashgate Publishing, 2003.

Henke, Ernst. "Andreae, Jacob," *Allgemeine Deutsche Biographie*, vol. 1. Leipzig: Duncker & Humblot, 1875.

Hone, William, ed. *The Lost Books of the Bible*. New York: Bell Publishing Company, 1979.

Hubben, William. *Dostoevsky, Kierkegaard, Nietzsche, and Kafka: Four Prophets of Our Destiny*. New York: Collier Books, 1962.

Kainz, Howard P. *G. W. F. Hegel*. Athens, Ohio: Ohio University Press, 1996.

Koester, Robert. *The Spirit of Pietism*. Milwaukee: Northwestern Publishing House, 2013.

Kolb, Robert, and James A. Nestingen, ed. *Sources and Contents of The Book of Concord*. Minneapolis: Fortress Press, 2001.

Labron, Tim. *Bultmann Unlocked*. London: T&T Clark, 2011.

Lalor, Stephen. *Matthew Tindal, Freethinker: An Eighteenth-century Assault on Religion*. London: Continuum International Publishing Group Ltd., 2006.

Leff, Gordon. *John Wyclif: The Path of Dissent*. Oxford: Oxford University Press, 1966.

Lucie-Smith, Edward. *Joan of Arc*. Bristol: Allen Lane, 1976.

Lützow, Count. *Life & Times of Master John Hus*. London: E. P. Dutton & Co., 1909.

Mann, William J. *Life and Times of Henry Melchior Muhlenberg*. Philadelphia: G.W. Frederick. 1888.

Manschreck, Clyde L. *Melanchthon: The Quiet Reformer*. New York: Abingdon Press, 1958.

Marsh, Charles. *Strange Glory: A Life of Dietrich Bonhoeffer*. New York: Knopf, 2014.

McCain, Paul T., Edward A. Engelbrecht, Robert C. Baker and Gene E. Veith, eds. *Concordia – The Lutheran Confessions*, 2nd ed. Translated by William H. T. Dau and Gerhard F. Bente. Saint Louis: Concordia Publishing House, 2006.

Metro Goldwyn Maier. *Luther*. Hollywood, California: 2003, (Movie).

Minus, Paul M. *Walter Rauschenbusch: American Reformer*. New York: Macmillan Publishing Company, 1988.

Moorman, John R. H. *Saint Francis of Assisi*. St. Bonaventure, New York: Franciscan Institute Publications, 1987.

Mueller, David Livingstone. *An Introduction to the Theology of Albrecht Ritschl*. London: Westminster Press, 1969.

O'Malley, John W. *Trent: What Happened at the Council*. Cambridge, Massachusetts: The Belknap Press of Harvard University Press, 2013.

Neusner, Jacob, ed. *The Babylonian Talmud: A Translation and Commentary*. Hendrickson Publishers, Inc., Peabody MA, 2005.

Percival, Henry R., ed. *The Seven Ecumenical Councils of the Undivided Church*. Peabody, Massachusetts: Hendrickson Publishers, 2004.

Preus, J. A. O. *The Second Martin: The Life and Theology of Martin Chemnitz*. Saint Louis: Concordia Publishing House, 1994.

Preus, Robert D. *The theology of Post-Reformation Lutheranism*, Vol. 1. Saint Louis: Concordia Publishing House, 1970.

Rees, Brinley, ed. *Pelagius: Life and Letters*. Woodbridge: The Boydell Press, 1991.

Roberts, Alexander and James Donaldson, eds. *Ante-Nicene Fathers*, Vols. 1-10. Peabody, Massachusetts: Hendrickson Publishers, 2002.

Sattler, Gary R. *God's Glory, Neighbor's Good: A brief introduction to the life and writings of August Hermann Francke*. Chicago: Covenant Press, 1982.

Schaff, Philip. *History of the Christian Church*, Vols. 1–8. Peabody, Massachusetts: Hendrickson Publishers, 2002.

Schmeling, Timothy, ed. *Lives and Writing of the Great Fathers of the Lutheran Church*. Saint Louis: Concordia Publishing House, 2016.

Schwiebert, Ernest G. *Luther and His Times*. Saint Louis: Concordia Publishing House, 1950.

Spade, Paul. *The Cambridge Companion to Ockham*. Cambridge: Cambridge University Press, 1999.

Stoeffler, F. Ernest, ed. *Continental Pietism and Early American Christianity*. Grand Rapids: Eerdmans, 1976.

Stump, Philip. *The Reforms of the Council of Constance (1414–1418)*. Boston: Brill Publishers, 1994.

Suelflow, August Robert. *Servant of the Word: The Life and Ministry of C.F.W. Walther*. Saint Louis: Concordia Publishing House, 2001.

Tedford, John. *The Life of John Wesley*. New York: Eaton & Mains, 1885.

Todd, Anne M. *Mohandas Gandhi*. New York: Infobase Publishing, 2009.

Unicorn Video. *Martin Luther*. Canoga Park, California (Movie).

Virgil. *The Aeneid*. Translated by Johann Grüninger. Franklin Center, Pennsylvania: The Franklin Library, 1982.

Voss, A. P., ed. *Continuing in His Word*. Milwaukee: Northwestern Publishing House, 1951.

Wade, Ira O. *Studies on Voltaire*. New York: Russell & Russell, 1967.

Wallmann, Johannes. *Philipp Jakob Spener und die Anfänge des Pietismus*, 2nd ed. Tübingen, Mohr Siebeck, 1970.

Ward, Maisie. *Saint Jerome*. London: Sheed & Ward, 1950.

Wellman, Sam. *Frederick the Wise: Seen and Unseen Lives of Martin Luther's Protector*. Mequon, Wisconsin: Wisconsin Lutheran Seminary Press, 2015.

Wolter, Allan B. *The Philosophical Theology of John Duns Scotus*. Ithaca: Cornell University Press, 1990.

Further Study

Below are college-level courses, collectively entitled *The Great Courses*, created by The Teaching Company located in Chantilly, Virginia, which give background information for topics covered in this book. The information is current, the lecturers are well recognized in their respective fields, and the courses are available in video format, audio format or by online subscription.

Aldrete, Gregory S. *The Roman Empire from Augustus to the Fall of Rome*, 2019.

Armstrong, Dorsey. *The Black Death – The World's Most Devastating Plague*, 2016.

———. *The Medieval World*, 2009.

Carlson, W. Bernard. *Understanding the Inventions That Changed the World*, 2013.

Cook, William R., and Ronald B. Herzman, *The Confessions of St Augustine*, 2004.

Daileader, Philip. *The Early Middle Ages*, 2004.

———. *The High Middle Ages*, 2001.

———. *The Late Middle Ages*, 2007.

Damrosch, Leo. *The History of the Decline and Fall of the Roman Empire*, 2017.

Gearon, Eamonn. *Turning Points in Middle Eastern History*, 2016.

Harl, Kenneth W. *The Vikings*, 2005.

Mathewes, Charles. *The City of God*, 2016.

Noble, Thomas F. X. *Popes and the Papacy: A History*, 2006.

Wolfson, Richard. *Einstein's Relatively and the Quantum Revolution: Modern Physics for Non-Scientists*, 2nd ed., 2000.

INDEX